Dorothy Wordsworth's
Illustrated
LAKELAND JOURNALS

Dorothy Wordsworth's
Illustrated
LAKELAND JOURNALS

Introduction by Rachel Trickett

Collins

First published 1987 by
William Collins Sons & Co Ltd
London·Glasgow·Sydney
Auckland·Toronto·Johannesburg

Conceived, designed and produced by Robert Ditchfield Ltd

British Library Cataloguing in Publication Data

Wordsworth, Dorothy
    Dorothy Wordsworth's illustrated Lakeland
    journals.
    1. Wordsworth, Dorothy — Biography
    2. Authors, English — 19th century —
    Biography
    I. Title
    828'.709   PR5849.A8
    ISBN 0-00-412263-1

Title page illustration: *Windermere, by Francis Wheatley*

Typeset by Oxford Computer Typesetting
Printed and bound in Hong Kong by Mandarin Offset

CONTENTS

In December 1799, Dorothy Wordsworth, then aged 27, and her brother, William, a year and a half older, moved to Dove Cottage, Grasmere in the English Lakeland. The following year, Dorothy began a personal journal which she kept until January 1803. She had no thought of it ever being published, but since it first appeared in 1897 it has established her reputation as one of the most remarkable and distinguished writers about life in the English countryside.

Dorothy Wordsworth (aged 62), by S. Crosthwaite

INTRODUCTION

The Wordsworths, like the Coleridges, the Brontës and the Tennysons, were among those remarkable nineteenth-century families of the professional middle-class (more especially of the Church), who in this period to some extent usurped the place of the aristocratic dynasties of earlier times in their influence on society. Each of them produced an outstanding writer, together with other talented siblings who made their mark in the academic world, the Church, the Law and the Armed Forces. Apart from the exceptional trio of Brontë sisters, however, only William and Dorothy Wordsworth represent the peculiarly intense imaginative bond and personal sympathy of kinship, which not only opened them to the friendship of Coleridge for a short but deeply influential period, but made the poet's best work, as he was ready enough to admit, almost like a collaboration between them.

The Wordsworth children were orphaned at an early age. Dorothy was born on Christmas Day 1771. She had two elder brothers, Richard and William, and was followed by two younger, John and Christopher. Their father, John Wordsworth, was a lawyer and agent to Lord Lowther. Their mother, Anne Cookson, died when Dorothy was six and she was fostered at Halifax by her mother's cousin Elizabeth Threlkeld. Her father died five years after his wife, in 1783, his financial affairs in some disorder because of a debt owed to him by his employer, and for the sake of economy Dorothy was removed from her happy second home in Halifax to live with her maternal grandparents in Penrith. This was a dismal time for her except for the visits of her brothers from Hawkshead grammar school, and she did not disguise it in her early letters to her friend Jane Pollard in Yorkshire. These letters give us some idea, too, of her education and reading; she was brought up in the tradition of the late eighteenth-century blue-stockings and the Dissenters and evangelicals of that age — her reading was in Mrs. Barbauld, Hannah More, Doddridge the Independent divine's sermons and hymns, and the works of Hayley, Blake's and Cowper's friend. She read, too, Richardson's *Clarissa,* a great favourite with her for its intricacy and sensibility, Fielding, Goldsmith and Milton.

Life in her grandparents' house, however, was dour and repressive, but from this she was rescued by the intervention of their son, William Cookson, then a fellow of St. John's College, Cambridge, who, on his marriage and his father's death in 1788 took up the college living of Forncett St. Peter in Norfolk and invited her to come and live with them there. In her days as the Rector's niece, Dorothy Wordsworth lived the life of a young woman devoted to good works and evangelical piety. That she was happy here there is no doubt from her letters and her obvious affection for her uncle and his wife, but there is little evidence — except for her warm emotional sensibility — of the independent spirit and the original imagination that her *Journals* were so soon to exhibit. She was a woman who quickly took on the colouring of her environment and her companions, especially if she loved them, and this was to be true of her throughout her life. It was at once her strength and her limitation.

Her brother William, then an undergraduate at St. John's College, Cambridge, began at this stage to play a peculiarly important part in her life. Awkward, brusque in his manner, but deeply emotional and affectionate, he was destined by his family for the Church, but had already doubts about this vocation. He had visited Forncett in 1790 and the instinctive affinity between him and Dorothy which they had felt in childhood was confirmed by their mutual confidences at this stage. In 1791 Wordsworth left for France and did not return to England until December 1792. During this time he had fallen in love with Annette Vallon, had been first fired, and then frightened by the violence of the Revolution, had become the father of Annette's child, and returned to London in a state of frustrated anxiety and divided political sentiments.

Dorothy, still in early 1793 writing to her friend Jane about her hopes of joining William in some rural parsonage, learned in February 1793 about William's French mistress and his child; and the strength of character, unconventionality and devotion to her brother which were to be so marked an aspect of her personality until middle age, at once were demonstrated. She left for Halifax and joined William there, walking with him in their native Lake District, and planned to live with him as his companion and housekeeper at the first opportunity. This came when Wordsworth's Cambridge friend, Raisley Calvert, with whom they had stayed in Keswick, died and left him a legacy which specifically enabled him to invest some money for his sister so that she could live with him. Another friend, Basil Montagu, told them of a house in Dorset belonging to the family of a radical acquaintance, John Pinney, which was offered to them for rent. To this they went, agreeing to bring up and care for Montagu's two-year-old son, as a further source of income and a chance to put into practice William's Rousseauean principles of education. Here to Racedown Lodge they came with the child in September 1795, and it was here that the deep imaginative intimacy between brother and sister first began to show its effect on Wordsworth's genius.

In his distracted condition, anxious over Annette and his child, over political ideals and poetic ambitions, Wordsworth came under the influence of his sister — of her spontaneity, her devotion, but most of all of her extraordinary sensibility to the minutiae at once of nature and of the details of ordinary life.

> She, whom I have loved
> With such communion, that no place on earth
> Can ever be a solitude to me . . .

insensibly became to him the necessary inspiration of his new and original poetry. Already, in *Descriptive Sketches* and *An Evening Walk* Wordsworth had shown his ability to imitate the late eighteenth-century form of the excursion poem, a meditative celebration of the beauty of the natural scene, with descriptive passages interspersing didactic reflections — discursive poetry of the kind Goldsmith and Cowper had perfected. Now he began to make out of the occasions of their everyday existence shorter and more immediate poems reflecting Dorothy's own delighted response to the incidents and occasions they shared in their new life together. In one of the poems composed in 1802 (a time of intense creativity for Wordsworth) he recalled the incident of finding a glow-worm and bringing it home to her at Racedown, returning from a visit to Lyme:

Dove Cottage early in the nineteenth century

> Among all lovely things my Love had been;
> Had noted well the stars, all flowers that grew
> About her home; but she had never seen
> A Glow-worm, never one, and this I knew . . .

The verses describe his careful carrying the glow-worm on a leaf through the storm and putting it under a tree in her garden, hoping that the next night it would shine:

> The whole next day I hoped, and hoped with fear;
> At night the Glow-worm shone beneath the tree;
> I led my Emma to the spot, 'Look here!'
> Oh! Joy it was for her, and joy for me!

This poem reads like one of Dorothy's own *Journal* entries in its poignancy, directness and simplicity and, describing an event which happened before she even began to transcribe her own impressions, indicates the nature of the relationship between brother and sister: mysterious, based on more than blood-kinship, and deeply bound up with the imaginative ties and affinities which connected them more permanently than even Wordsworth's flawed attachment to Coleridge — 'the only wonderful man I ever knew' — or his passionate, more recognisable love for his wife, Mary.

It was at Racedown that Coleridge found them, jumping over the hedge and erupting into their lives.

'Wordsworth and his exquisite Sister are with me' he wrote to Cottle. 'She is a woman indeed! — in mind, I mean, and heart — for her person is such, that if you expected to see a pretty woman you would think her ordinary — if you expected to find an ordinary woman you would think her pretty! — But her manners are simple, ardent, impressive . . . . Her information various — her eye watchful in minutest observation of nature — and her taste a perfect electrometer — it bends, protrudes, and draws in at subtlest beauties and most recondite faults.'

Dorothy would not have recognized herself in this subtle and vivid description, but the admiration was mutual and from this point to their residence at Alfoxden in Somerset to which they moved shortly to be near Coleridge, the extraordinary inter-relationship between the three of them continued in a period of rich creativity for each. The early *Lyrical Ballads, The Ancient Mariner, Kubla Khan* and the beginnings of Dorothy's *Journal* belong to this *annus mirabilis,* but Coleridge's Conversation poems (written in that meditative tradition of late eighteenth-century verse which suited his genius better than Wordsworth's) — especially *The Nightingale* — give us an intimate picture of their united sensibilities, their conversation together, and their varied responsiveness which is more vivid than anything except Dorothy's *Journal* itself.

The Alfoxden entries which begin in 1798 already show her vividness of perception: 'the ivy twisting round the oaks like bristled serpents'; 'the half-dead sound of the near sheep-bell, in the hollow of the sloping coombe, exquisitely soothing'; 'walked with Coleridge over the hills . . . gathered sticks in the wood; a perfect stillness. The redbreasts sang upon the leafless boughs . . . the moonlight still and warm as a summer's night at nine o'clock'. 'Met a razor-grinder with a soldier's jacket on, a knapsack on his back, and a boy to drag his wheel. The sea very black and making a loud noise as we came through the wood, loud as if disturbed, and the wind was silent.' 'William and I drank tea at Coleridge's. A cloudy sky . . . One only leaf upon the top of a tree — the sole remaining leaf — danced round and round like a rag blown by the wind'. 'The sole red leaf, the last of its clan' of *Christabel* comes to mind here, and her instant perception of silence or stillness recalls *Frost at Midnight* with its evocation of 'extreme silentness'.

But the fullness of Dorothy Wordsworth's imagination does not reveal itself until the *Grasmere Journals.* In them we discover not only her delicacy of imaginative perception, but her intensity of mood, her instinctive sympathy and interest in ordinary people — the vagrants, beggars, travellers who pass through her brother's poems, and the children with whom she felt an immediate affinity. In 1799 on December 20th Dorothy and William Wordsworth arrived at Dove Cottage, Grasmere, which was to be their home till 1808. The best years of Dorothy's life were spent here, especially when she was alone with her brother (though aware of his need to marry, and his intention to marry their old childhood friend, Mary Hutchinson, who came often to visit them), and could share with him to an extraordinary degree the experience of reading and composing poetry. Hers was a strenuous life, and it is astonishing to discover how much time she could afford after domestic chores for walking, reading and transcribing her brother's poems. She was already secure in the knowledge of what she had meant to him in the development of his imagination, though there is no suggestion in the *Journal* that she thought of herself except in the humblest sense of

William Wordsworth (aged 28), by W. Shuter

companion and transcriber, as a 'Muse'. But he had written the conclusion of *Tintern Abbey* and she could not have missed the fervour in the lines

> In thy voice I catch
> The language of my former heart, and read
> My former pleasures in the shooting lights
> Of thy wild eyes. Oh! — yet a little while
> May I behold in thee what I was once,
> My dear, dear Sister!

In the entries of the *Grasmere Journal* Dorothy's devotion to her brother is the predominant theme. He was frequently ill (as she was); composition brought on pains and headaches; they tramped over the hills to Keswick to see the Southeys and Coleridges; entertained the Hutchinsons; survived together the upheavals that disturbed Wordsworth so much at the time of the Peace of Amiens when he and Dorothy (knowing that he intended to marry Mary) went over to France to see Annette and his daughter. And all this time Dorothy's own sense of inevitable loss of that sole companionship which had come to mean so much to her imaginatively as well as personally never precluded her snail-horn perceptions, or her interest in the ordinary life that surrounded her. If it was a time of distress for Wordsworth, it was also a time of great creativity, and there is no doubt that this was made possible by Dorothy's presence. So the entries in her *Journal* for this whole period have a peculiar interest, and the danger is that we read them more in relation to him and his development than to her. Her own modesty, and the fact that so many of the incidents she records — the meeting with the Beggar woman and her children, with the Leech Gatherer, the sight of the daffodils at Ullswater — were the origin of some of his finest poems, hinder our reading the *Journal* as an independent work of the imagination. So she would have wished it, but so he would not. Wordsworth's distractions differed from Coleridge's in that he did not need a perpetual reflection of his ideal sense of self as a symbol of love. That he saw in his younger sister what he was once did not not blind him to the independent and objective existence of someone so dear to him. Though he could write to his wife Mary 'the blessed bond that binds husband and wife so much closer than the bond of Brotherhood — however dear', and though it is embarrassing to find him asking Mary to excuse him for deleting too loving phrases in their letters in case they offend Dorothy, he could write of her, as Coleridge could not of any woman, when he dreaded her death, 'were she to depart the Phasis of my Moon would be robbed of light to a degree that I have not courage to think of.'

The *Grasmere Journal* needs no quotation to recommend it. It is full of familiar and marvellous entries — not only those that constitute the origin of Wordsworth's poems, but many others that reveal Dorothy's own sensibility and her responsiveness to the people among whom she lived. We learn of Molly, the old servant, of her and William's reading together of Chaucer, Milton and Jonson, of her own reading of Shakespeare; the garden she so much loved, with its vegetables as well as the roses and honeysuckle — utility and beauty combined; especially, too, the birds Dorothy cared for above all. Everywhere she looked she loved, and her associations of places with people spring as naturally to her mind as most people's association of places with maps and holidays:

The Birches on the crags beautiful. Red brown and glittering — the ashes glittering spears with their upright stems — the hips very beautiful, and so good!! and dear Coleridge — I ate twenty for thee when I was by myself. I came home first — they walked too slow for me.

The *Journal* ends with William's marriage. Again Dorothy expresses quite simply her emotions (though reference to the ring was later deleted):

At a little after 8 o'clock I saw them go down the avenue towards the church. William had parted from me upstairs. I gave him the wedding ring — with how deep a blessing! I took it from my forefinger where I had worn it the whole of the night before — he slipped it again upon my finger and blessed me fervently.

Two months later one of the last *Journal* entries captures for us the future rhythm of their lives:

December 24th 1802, Christmas Eve: William is now sitting by me at ½ past 10 o'clock. I have been beside him ever since tea running the heel of a stocking, repeating some of his sonnets to him, listening to his own repeating, reading some of Milton's, and the Allegro and Penseroso. It is a quiet keen frost. Mary is in the parlour below attending to the baking of cakes and Jenny Fletcher's pies. Sara is in bed with the toothache, and so we are — beloved William is turning over the leaves of Charlotte Smith's sonnets . . .

This entry with its mingling of snugness and discomfort looks forward to the sad and all too human conclusion of the story. Coleridge and De Quincey felt that Wordsworth had not benefited from the adulation of three women — his wife Mary, her sister Sara (Coleridge's Asra) and Dorothy. Their roles in his life were, indeed, very different from the free and independent part that Dorothy had played in the years in which her *Journal* had been kept. The painful estrangement from Coleridge (though as much his fault as Wordsworth's) revealed the breach that had widened after Wordsworth's marriage. Dorothy, the exquisite sister, would not go to see Coleridge or mend the break from a narrow loyalty to her brother; later her coldness to De Quincey after his marriage to a local girl of whom the Wordsworths disapproved, influenced his description of the family. She threw herself into the role of protector of William's children in a fashion that embarrasses present day readers of her letters and must have equally embarrassed her correspondents. Though she retained her spontaneity and sensibility enough to captivate later friends like Henry Crabb Robinson, and to ensure the love of older ones like Catherine Clarkson, she narrowed her circle more and more.

A Sketch by John Harden of Dorothy Wordsworth in her early seventies

Samuel Taylor Coleridge, by P. Vandyke

The end of her life was cruel indeed — twenty years of senility during which her brother and his long-suffering wife protected and nursed her — a return on his part, which he never regretted, of the debt he owed to her, but it is a sad supplement to the radiant early years which this *Journal* records.

Yet this tragic conclusion, lasting so long, should not blind us to the truth which the *Journal* and Wordsworth's poems reveal. 'She gave me eyes, she gave me ears' he wrote of her, and remembered from their childhood the two of them chasing butterflies — he intent on the prey — 'But she, God love her, feared to brush the dust from off its wings.' That marvellous tribute derives from a simple reminiscence, of the kind Dorothy's *Journal* is full of, and of which, perhaps, this is the most perfect example:

William had slept badly — he got up at 9 o'clock, but before he rose finished with Beggar Boys — and while we were at Breakfast that is (for I had breakfasted) he, with his Basin of Broth before him untouched and a little plate of Bread and butter he wrote the Poem to a Butterfly. He ate not a morsel, nor put on his stockings but sate with his shirt neck unbuttoned and his waistcoat open while he did it. The thought came first upon him as we were talking about the pleasure we both always feel at the sight of a Butterfly. I told him that I used to chase them a little but that I was afraid of brushing the dust of their wings and did not catch them — He told me how they used to kill all the white ones when he went to school because they were frenchmen. Mr. Simpson came in just as he was finishing the Poem. After he was gone I wrote it down and the other poems and I read them all over to him.

In this innocent entry, with all that it reveals, we can see both Dorothy Wordsworth's exceptional qualities, and what they had given to her brother. The *Journal* survives not only as a tribute to what he received from her, which he repayed whole-heartedly, but as the record of a unique sensibility — her own — which is responded to by readers she would never have thought would even know her name.

Rachel Trickett

THE CHARACTERS

The ASHBURNER family lived in a small cottage opposite the Wordsworths. Thomas Ashburner's first wife, Anne, had died in 1791 and later that year he had married Margaret Lancaster ('Peggy'). There had been five daughters by the first marriage — Agnes (born 1781), Anne (1783), Jane (1786), Mary (1788) and Sara (1790).

FRANK BATEMAN ('Baty') lived a little up the hill from Dove Cottage, on the other side of the road.

MR. BENSON lived at Tail End. It was from him that the Wordsworths rented Dove Cottage.

WILLIAM CALVERT was a friend of William's and brother of Raisley Calvert, whose legacy had given William his independence.

THOMAS CLARKSON (1760–1846) and his wife Catherine lived during the period of the *Journals* at Eusemere, at the north end of Ullswater. Thomas was a prominent anti-slavery campaigner.

SAMUEL TAYLOR COLERIDGE (1772–1834) — please see the Introduction.

JOHN FISHER (born 1746), his wife Agnes ('Aggy') and sister Mary ('Molly', born 1741) lived in the house opposite Dove Cottage, known as Sykeside. John often helped the Wordsworths with gardening and odd jobs, and Molly, who was nearly sixty years old when the Wordsworths arrived at Dove Cottage, was their devoted help about the house. John and Agnes had a son, also John, who was born in 1778 and is mentioned in the *Journals* on June 21, 1802.

FLETCHER the carrier, who brought letters to and from Keswick, kept his horses at Town End. 'He seems machanized to labour.' (February 8, 1802).

The HUTCHINSON family — please see the Introduction.

CHARLES LLOYD (1775–1839) was a poet and friend of Coleridge who had moved with his new wife to Old Brathay, near Ambleside, in 1800. Charles's sister, Priscilla, was engaged to Dorothy's brother, Christopher.

CAPTAIN and MRS LUFF were friends of the Clarksons.

GAWEN MACKARETH ('Goan', born 1745) and his wife, Mary, lived at Lane End, which was probably near Knott Houses to the north of the village. They had five children, the last of whom was born in 1801 but who, as Dorothy mentions on June 3 and 6 1802, fell ill and died in infancy. George Mackareth (brother of Gawen, born 1752) lived at Knott Houses. The Wordsworths would send to him when they needed to hire a horse. Three of his children are referred to in the *Journals* — George (born 1780), Ellen (1789) and William (1791).

JOHN OLLIFF and his wife lived at the Hollins, and Dorothy often refers to the wood and field that belonged to them. A son, George, was born in 1798, a daughter in February 1802, but the baby died the following month.

JOHN SIMPSON had married Mary Park in 1794 and the couple lived with her parents at Nab Cottage, which had been in the Park family since 1332. They had six children — Margaret ('Peggy', born 1796), John (1797), William (1801), Mary (1803), Anne (1806) and Elizabeth (1808). In 1817 Margaret married Thomas de Quincey.

The Sympson family (usually written 'Simpson' in the *Journals*) lived at Broadrain and the Wordsworths clearly spent much time in their company. The Revd Joseph Sympson was vicar at Wythburn for more than fifty years and died in 1807 at the age of 92; his wife, Mary, in 1806 at the age of 81. Their daughter, Elizabeth Jane, married in 1803 but died the following year at the age of 37 after the birth of a daughter, who herself survived only to the end of the year. Two other daughters are mentioned in the *Journals* — Mary and Jenny, and three sons — Joseph, a clergyman like his father, Bartholomew and Robert.

Annette Vallon and her daughter, Caroline — please see the Introduction.

Cottage Group, by W. H. Pyne

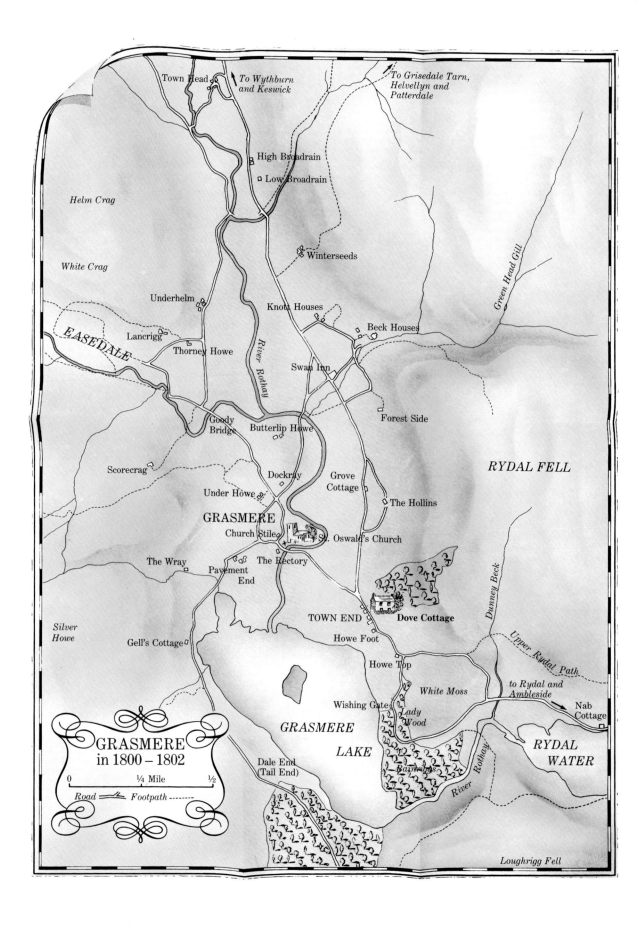

Town Head

To Wythburn and Keswick

To Grisedale Tarn, Helvellyn and Patterdale

High Broadrain

Low Broadrain

Helm Crag

White Crag

Winterseeds

Green Head Gill

Underhelm

Knott Houses

Beck Houses

EASEDALE

Lancrigg

Thorney Howe

River Rothay

Swan Inn

Goody Bridge

Butterlip Howe

Forest Side

RYDAL FELL

Scorecrag

Dockray

Grove Cottage

The Hollins

Under Howe

GRASMERE

Church Stile

St. Oswald's Church

The Wray

Pavement End

The Rectory

Dunney Beck

Silver Howe

TOWN END

Dove Cottage

Gell's Cottage

Howe Foot

Howe Top

White Moss

Upper Rydal Path

to Rydal and Ambleside

Nab Cottage

Wishing Gate

Lady Wood

GRASMERE

LAKE

River Rothay

RYDAL WATER

Dale End (Tail End)

Bainriggs

Loughrigg Fell

GRASMERE
in 1800 – 1802

0   ¼ Mile   ½

Road   Footpath

I. *May 14th to December 22nd, 1800*

May 14th, 1800 [*Wednesday*]. Wm. and John set off into Yorkshire after dinner at ½ past 2 o'clock, cold pork in their pockets. I left them at the turning of the Lowwood bay under the trees. My heart was so full that I could hardly speak to W. when I gave him a farewell kiss. I sate a long time upon a stone at the margin of the lake, and after a flood of tears my heart was easier. The lake looked to me, I knew not why, dull and melancholy, and the weltering on the shores seemed a heavy sound. I walked as long as I could amongst the stones of the shore. The wood rich in flowers; a beautiful yellow, palish yellow, flower, that looked thick, round, and double, and smelt very sweet — I supposed it was a ranunculus. Crowfoot, the grassy-leaved rabbit-toothed white flower, strawberries, geranium, scentless violets, anemones two kinds, orchises, primroses. The heckberry very beautiful, the crab coming out as a low shrub. Met a blind man, driving a very large beautiful Bull, and a cow — he walked with two sticks. Came home by Clappersgate. The valley very green; many sweet views up to Rydale head, when I could juggle away the fine houses; but they disturbed me, even more than when I have been happier; one beautiful view of the Bridge, without Sir Michael's.[1] Sate down very often, though it was cold. I resolved to write a journal of the time till W. and J. return, and I set about keeping my resolve, because I will not quarrel with

1. *i.e.* Rydal Hall, the seat of Sir Michael le Fleming.

myself, and because I shall give Wm. pleasure by it when he comes home again. At Rydale, a woman of the village, stout and well dressed, begged a half-penny; she had never she said done it before, but these hard times! Arrived at home with a bad headach, set some slips of privett, the evening cold, had a fire, my face now flame-coloured. It is nine o'clock. I shall soon go to bed. A young woman begged at the door — she had come from Manchester on Sunday morn. with two shillings and a slip of paper which she supposed a Bank note — it was a cheat. She had buried her husband and three children within a year and a half — all in one grave — burying very dear — paupers all put in one place — 20 shillings paid for as much ground as will bury a man — a stone to be put over it or the right will be lost — 11/6 each time the ground is opened. Oh! that I had a letter from William!

May 15th, Thursday. A coldish dull morning — hoed the first row of peas, weeded etc. etc., sat hard to mending till evening. The rain which had threatened all day came on just when I was going to walk.

[*May 16th,*] *Friday morning.* Warm and mild, after a fine night of rain. Transplanted radishes after breakfast, walked to Mr. Gell's with the books, gathered mosses and plants. The woods extremely beautiful with all autumnal variety and softness. I carried a basket for mosses, and gathered some wild plants. Oh! that we had a book of botany. All flowers now are gay and deliciously sweet. The primrose still pre-eminent among the later flowers of the spring. Foxgloves very tall, with their heads budding. I went forward round the lake at the foot of

Loughrigg Fell. I was much amused with the business of a pair of stone-chats; their restless voices as they skimmed along the water following each other, their shadows under them, and their returning back to the stones on the shore, chirping with the same unwearied voice. Could not cross the water, so I went round by the stepping-stones. The morning clear but cloudy, that is the hills were not over-hung by mists. After dinner Aggy weeded onions and carrots. I helped for a little — wrote to Mary Hutchinson — washed my head — worked. After tea went to Ambleside — a pleasant cool but not cold evening. Rydale was very beautiful, with spear-shaped streaks of polished steel. No letters! — only one newspaper. I returned by Clappersgate. Grasmere was very solemn in the last glimpse of twilight; it calls home the heart to quietness. I had been very melancholy in my walk back. I had many of my saddest thoughts, and I could not keep the tears within me. But when I came to Grasmere I felt that it did me good. I finished my letter to M. H. Ate hasty pudding and went to bed. As I was going out in the morning I met a half crazy old man. He shewed me a pincushion and begged a pin, afterwards a half-penny. He began in a kind of indistinct voice in this manner: "Matthew Jobson's lost a cow. Tom Nichol has two good horses strayed. Jim Jones's cow's brokken her horn, etc. etc." He went into Aggy's and persuaded her to give him some whey, and let him boil some porridge. She declares he ate two quarts.

[*May* 17*th,*] *Saturday.* Incessant rain from morning till night. T. Ashburner brought us coals. Worked hard, and read *Midsummer Night's Dream,* [and] Ballads — sauntered a little in the garden. The Skobby[1] sate quietly in its nest, rocked by the wind, and beaten by the rain.

1. Skobby, dialect for chaffinch.

[*May*] 18*th, Sunday.* Went to church, slight showers, a cold air. The mountains from this window look much greener, and I think the valley is more green than ever. The corn begins to shew itself. The ashes are still bare, went part of the way

Grasmere Church and Bridge, by Thomas Austin

home with Miss Simpson. A little girl from Coniston came to beg. She had lain out all night — her step-mother had turned her out of doors. Her father could not stay at home "she flights so". Walked to Ambleside in the evening round the lake, the prospect exceedingly beautiful from Loughrigg Fell. It was so green that no eye could be weary of reposing upon it. The most beautiful situation for a house in the field next to Mr. Benson's. It threatened rain all the evening but was mild and pleasant. I was overtaken by 2 Cumberland people on the other side of Rydale who complimented me upon my walking. They were going to sell cloth, and odd things which they make themselves, in Hawkshead and the neighbourhood. The post was not arrived, so I walked thro' the town, past Mrs. Taylor's, and met him. Letters from Coleridge and Cottle. John Fisher overtook me on the other side of Rydale. He talked much about the alteration in the times, and observed that in a short time there would be only two ranks of people, the very rich and the very poor, "for those who have small estates", says he, "are forced to sell, and all the land goes into one hand". Did not reach home till 10 o'clock.

[*May 19th,*] *Monday.* Sauntered a good deal in the garden, bound carpets, mended old clothes. Read *Timon of Athens*. Dried linen. Molly weeded the turnips, John stuck the peas. We had not much sunshine or wind, but no rain till about 7 o'clock, when we had a slight shower just after I had set out upon my

The Market Place, Ambleside,
by J. C. Ibbetson

walk. I did not return but walked up into the Black Quarter.[1] I sauntered a long time among the rocks above the church. The most delightful situation possible for a cottage, commanding two distinct views of the

1. The Black Quarter, the name given by the W.s to Easedale, during their first year's residence at Grasmere.

vale and of the lake, is among those rocks. I strolled on, gathered mosses etc. The quietness and still seclusion of the valley affected me even to producing the deepest melancholy. I forced myself from it. The wind rose before I went to bed. No rain — Dodwell and Wilkinson called in my absence.

[*May 20th,*] *Tuesday Morning.* A fine mild rain. After breakfast the sky cleared and before the clouds passed from the hills I went to Ambleside. It was a sweet morning. Everything green and overflowing with life, and the streams making a perpetual song, with the thrushes and all little birds, not forgetting the stonechats. The post was not come in. I walked as far as Windermere, and met him there. No letters! no papers. Came home by Clappersgate. I was sadly tired, ate a hasty dinner and had a bad headach — went to bed and slept at least 2 hours. Rain came on in the evening — Molly washing.

[*May 21st,*] *Wednesday.* Went often to spread the linen which was bleaching — a rainy day and very wet night.

[*May 22nd,*] *Thursday.* A very fine day with showers — dried the linen and starched. Drank tea at Mr. Simpson's. Brought down Batchelor's Buttons (Rock Ranunculus) and other plants — went part of the way back, a showery mild evening — all the peas up.

[*May*] *23rd, Friday.* Ironing till tea time. So heavy a rain that I could not go for letters — put by the linen, mended stockings etc.

May 24th, Saturday. Walked in the morning to Ambleside. I found a letter from Wm. and from Mary Hutchinson and Douglas. Returned on the other side of the lakes — wrote to William after dinner, nailed up the beds, worked in the garden, sate in the evening under the trees. I went to bed soon with a bad headach. A fine day.

[*May 25th,*] *Sunday.* A very fine warm day, had no fire. Read *Macbeth* in the morning, sate under the trees after dinner. Miss Simpson came just as I was going out and she sate with me. I wrote to my brother Christopher, and sent John Fisher to Ambleside after tea. Miss Simpson and I walked to the foot of the lake — her Brother met us. I went with them nearly home and on my return found a letter from Coleridge and from Charles Lloyd, and three papers.

May 26th, Monday. A very fine morning, worked in the garden till after 10 when old Mr. Simpson came and talked to me till after 12. Molly weeding — wrote letters to J. H., Coleridge, C. Ll., and W. I walked towards Rydale, and turned aside at my favorite field. The air and the lake were still — one cottage light in the vale, and so much of day left that I could distinguish objects, the woods, trees and houses. Two or three different kinds of birds sang at intervals on the opposite shore. I sate till I could hardly drag myself away, I grew so sad. "When pleasant thoughts," etc. . . .

[*May*] *27th, Tuesday.* I walked to Ambleside with letters — met the post before

I reached Mr. Partridge's, one paper, only a letter for Coleridge. I expected a letter from Wm. It was a sweet morning, the ashes in the valley nearly in full leaf, but still to be distinguished, quite bare on the higher ground. I was warm in returning, and becoming cold with sitting in the house I had a bad headach — went to bed after dinner, and lay till after 5. Not well after tea. I worked in the garden, but did not walk further. A delightful evening before the sun set, but afterwards it grew colder — mended stockings etc.

[*May 28*th,] *Wednesday*. In the morning walked up to the rocks above Jenny Dockeray's, sate a long time upon the grass, the prospect divinely beautiful. If I had three hundred pounds, and could afford to have a bad interest for my money, I would buy that estate, and we would build a cottage there to end our days in. I went into her garden and got white and yellow lilies, periwinkle, etc., which I planted. Sate under the trees with my work. No fire in the morning. Worked till between 7 and 8, and then watered the garden, and was about to go up to Mr. Simpson's, when Miss S. and her visitors passed the door. I went home with them, a beautiful evening, the crescent moon hanging above Helm Crag.

[*May 29th,*] *Thursday*. In the morning worked in the garden a little, read *King John*. Miss Simpson, and Miss Falcon and Mr. S. came very early. Went to Mr.

Gell's boat before tea. We fished upon the lake, and amongst us caught 13 Bass. Miss Simpson brought gooseberries *and cream*. Left the water at near nine o'clock, very cold. Went part of the way home with the party.

[*May 30th,*] *Friday*. In the morning went to Ambleside, forgetting that the post does not come till the evening. How was I grieved when I was so informed. I walked back, resolving to go again in the evening. It rained very mildly and sweetly in the morning as I came home, but came on a wet afternoon and evening, but chilly. I caught Mr. Olliff's lad as he was going for letters, he brought me one from Wm. and 12 papers. I planted London Pride upon the well, and many things on the borders. John sodded the wall. As I came past Rydale in the morning, I saw a Heron swimming with only its neck out of water; it beat and struggled amongst the water, when it flew away, and was long in getting loose.

[*May 31st,*] *Saturday*. A sweet mild rainy morning. Grundy the carpet man called. I paid him 1-10/-. Went to the blind man's for plants. I got such a load that I was obliged to leave my basket in the road, and send Molly for it. Planted till after dinner when I was putting up vallances. Miss Simpson and her visitors called. I went with them to Brathay Bridge. We got Broom on returning, strawberries etc., came home by Ambleside. Grasmere looked divinely beautiful. Mr. and Miss Simpson and Tommy drank tea at 8 o'clock. I walked to the Potters with them.

Brathay Bridge, Old Brathay, by John Harden

The Old Mill, Ambleside, by James Burrell Smith

June 1st, Sunday. Rain in the night — a sweet mild morning. Read Ballads; went to church. Singers from Wytheburn, went part of the way home with Miss Simpson. Walked upon the hill above the house till dinner time — went again to church — Christening and singing which kept us very late. The pewside came down with me. Walked with Mr. Simpson nearly home. After tea, went to Ambleside, round the lakes — a very fine warm evening. I lay upon the steep of Loughrigg, my heart dissolved in what I saw, when I was not startled but re-called from my reverie by a noise as of a child paddling without shoes. I looked up and saw a lamb close to me. It approached nearer and nearer, as if to examine me, and stood a long time. I did not move. At last it ran past me, and went bleating along the pathway, seeming to be seeking its mother. I saw a hare on the high road. The post was not come in; waited in the road till John's apprentice came with a letter from Coleridge and 3 papers. The moon shone upon the water — reached home at 10 o'clock, went to bed immediately. Molly brought daisies etc. which we planted.

[*June 2nd,*] *Monday.* A cold dry windy morning. I worked in the garden, and planted flowers, etc. Sate under the trees after dinner till tea time. John Fisher stuck the peas, Molly weeded and washed. I went to Ambleside after tea, crossed the stepping-stones at the foot of Grasmere, and pursued my way on the other side of Rydale and by Clappersgate. I sate a long time to watch the hurrying waves, and to hear the regularly irregular sound of the dashing waters. The waves round about the little Island seemed like a dance of spirits that rose out of the water, round its small circumference of shore. Inquired about lodgings for Coleridge, and was accompanied by Mrs. Nicholson as far as Rydale. This was very kind, but God be thanked, I want not society by a moonlight lake. It was near 11 when I reached home. I wrote to Coleridge, and went late to bed.

[*June 3rd,*] *Tuesday.* I sent off my letter by the Butcher. A boisterous drying day. I worked in the garden before dinner. Read *R[ichar]d Second* — was not well after dinner and lay down. Mrs. Simpson's grandson brought me some gooseberries. I got up and walked with him part of the way home, afterwards went down rambling by the lake side — got Lockety Goldings, strawberries etc., and planted. After tea the wind fell. I walked towards Mr. Simpson's, gave the newspapers to the Girl, reached home at 10. No letter, no William — a letter from R[ichar]d to John.

[*June 4th,*] *Wednesday.* A very fine day. I sate out of doors most of the day, wrote to Mr. Jackson. Ambleside Fair. I walked to the lake-side in the morning, took up plants, and sate upon a stone reading Ballads. In the evening I was watering plants when Mr. and Miss Simpson called. I accompanied them home, and we went to the waterfall at the head of the valley. It was very interesting in the Twilight. I brought home lemon thyme, and several other plants, and planted them by moonlight. I lingered out of doors in the hope of hearing my Brother's tread.

[*June 5th,*] *Thursday*. I sate out of doors great part of the day and worked in the garden — had a letter from Mr. Jackson, and wrote an answer to Coleridge. The little birds busy making love, and pecking the blossoms and bits of moss off the trees; they flutter about and about, and thrid the trees as I lie under them. Molly went out to tea, I would not go far from home, expecting my Brothers. I rambled on the hill above the house, gathered wild thyme, and took up roots of wild columbine. Just as I was returning with my load, Mr. and Miss Simpson called. We went again upon the hill, got more plants, set them, and then went to the Blind Man's for London Pride for Miss Simpson. I went up with them as far as the Blacksmith's, a fine lovely moonlight night.

[*June 6th,*] *Friday*. Sate out of doors reading the whole afternoon, but in the morning I wrote to my aunt Cookson. In the evening I went to Ambleside with Coleridge's letter — it was a lovely night as the day had been. I went by Loughrigg and Clappersgate and just met the post at the turnpike; he told me there were two letters but none for me, so I was in no hurry and went round again by Clappersgate, crossed the stepping-stones and entered Ambleside at Matthew Harrison's. A letter from Jack Hutchinson, and one from Montagu, enclosing a 3£ note. No William! I slackened my pace as I came near home, fearing to hear that he was not come. I listened till after one o'clock to every barking dog, cock-fighting, and other sports: it was Mr. Borwick's opening. Foxgloves just coming into blossom.

[*June 7,*] *Saturday*. A very warm cloudy morning, threatening to rain. I walked

up to Mr. Simpson's to gather gooseberries — it was a very fine afternoon. Little Tommy came down with me, ate gooseberry pudding and drank tea with me. We went up the hill, to gather sods and plants, and went down to the lake side, and took up orchises, etc. I watered the garden and weeded. I did not leave home, in the expectation of Wm. and John, and sitting at work till after 11 o'clock I heard a foot go to the front of the house, turn round, and open the gate. It was William! After our first joy was over, we got some tea. We did not go to bed till 4 o'clock in the morning, so he had an opportunity of seeing our improvements. The birds were singing, and all looked fresh, though not gay. There was a greyness on earth and sky. We did not rise till near 10 in the morning. We were busy all day in writing letters to Coleridge, Montagu, Douglas, Richard. Mr. and Miss Simpson called in the evening, the little boy carried our letters to Ambleside. We walked with Mr. and Miss S. home, on their return. The evening was cold and I was afraid of the toothach for William. We met John on our return home.

[June] 9th, Monday. In the morning W. cut down the winter cherry tree. I sowed French beans and weeded. A coronetted Landau went by, when we were sitting upon the sodded wall. The ladies (evidently Tourists) turned an eye of interest upon our little garden and cottage. We went to R. Newton's for pike floats and went round to Mr. Gell's boat, and on to the lake to fish. We caught nothing — it was extremely cold. The reeds and bullrushes or bullpipes of a tender soft green, making a plain whose surface moved with the wind. The reeds not yet tall. The lake clear to the bottom, but saw no fish. In the evening I stuck peas, watered the garden, and planted brocoli. Did not walk, for its was very cold. A poor girl called to beg, who had no work at home, and was going in search of it to Kendal. She slept in Mr. Benson's [?], and went off after breakfast in the morning with 7d. and a letter to the Mayor of Kendal.

[June] 10th, Tuesday. A cold, yet sunshiny morning. John carried letters to Ambleside. I made tarts, pies, etc. Wm. stuck peas. After dinner he lay down. John not at home. I stuck peas alone. Molly washing. Cold showers with hail and

Above Grasmere, by John Harden

rain, but at half-past five, after a heavy rain, the lake became calm and very beautiful. Those parts of the water which were perfectly unruffled lay like green islands of various shapes. W. and I walked to Ambleside to seek lodgings for C. No letters. No papers. It was a very cold chearless evening. John had been fishing in Langdale and was gone to bed.

On Tuesday, May 27th, a very tall woman, tall much beyond the measure of tall women, called at the door. She had on a very long brown cloak and a very white cap, without bonnet; her face was excessively brown, but it had plainly once been fair. She led a little bare-footed child about 2 years old by the hand, and said her husband, who was a tinker, was gone before with the other children. I gave her a piece of bread. Afterwards on my road to Ambleside, beside the bridge at Rydale, I saw her husband sitting by the roadside, his two asses feeding beside him, and the two young children at play upon the grass. The man did not beg. I passed on and about ¼ of a mile further I saw two boys before me, one about 10, the other about 8 years old, at play chasing a butterfly. They were wild figures, not very ragged, but without shoes and stockings; the hat of the elder was wreathed round with yellow flowers, the younger whose hat was only a rimless crown, had stuck it round with laurel leaves. They continued at play till I drew very near, and then they addressed me with the begging cant and the whining voice of sorrow. I said "I served your mother this morning". (The Boys were so like the woman who had called at the door that I could not be mistaken.) "O!" says the elder, "you could not serve my mother for she's dead, and my father's on

Gipsies,

by W. H. Pyne

at the next town — he's a potter." I persisted in my assertion, and that I would give them nothing. Says the elder, "Come, let's away", and away they flew like lightning. They had however sauntered so long in their road that they did not reach Ambleside before me, and I saw them go up to Matthew Harrison's house with their wallet upon the elder's shoulder, and creeping with a beggar's complaining foot. On my return through Ambleside I met in the street the mother driving her asses; in the two panniers of one of which were the two little children, whom she was chiding and threatening with a wand which she used to drive on her asses, while the little things hung in wantonness over the pannier's edge. The woman had told me in the morning that she was of Scotland, which her accent fully proved, but that she had lived (I think) at Wigton, that they could not keep a house and so they travelled.

June 11th,[1] *Wednesday.* A very cold morning — we went on the lake to set pike floats with John's fish. W. and J. went first alone. Mr. Simpson called, and I accompanied him to the lake side. My Brothers and I again went upon the water, and returned to dinner. We landed upon the Island where I saw the whitest hawthorn I have seen this year, the generality of hawthorns are bloomless. I saw wild roses in the hedges. Went to bed in the afternoon and slept till after six — a threatening of the toothach. Wm. and John went to the pike floats — they brought in 2 pikes. I sowed kidney-beans and spinnach. A cold evening. Molly stuck the peas. I weeded a little. Did not walk.

[1]. This and the two following dates D. W. gives, incorrectly, as June 13, 14, and 15.

June 12th, Thursday. William and I went upon the water to set pike floats. John fished under Loughrigg. We returned to dinner, 2 pikes boiled and roasted. A very cold air but warm sun. W. and I again went upon the water. We walked to Rydale after tea, and up to potter's. A cold night, but warmer.

June 13th, Friday. A rainy morning. W. and J. went upon the Lake. Very warm, and pleasant gleams of sunshine. Went upon the water after tea, caught a pike 7½ [lbs.]. Mr. Simpson trolling. Mr. Gell and his party came.

[*June 14th,*] *Saturday.* A fine morning but cloudy. W. and John went upon the lake. I staid at home. We drank tea at Mr. Simpson's. Stayed till after 10 o'clock.

[*June 15th,*] *Sunday.* John walked to Coniston. W. and I sauntered in the garden. Afterwards walked by the lake side — a cold air. We pushed through the wood. Walked behind the fir grove, and returned to dinner. W. lay down after dinner, Parker, the Tanner and the blacksmith from Hawkshead called.

[*June 16th,*] *Monday.* Wm. and I went to Brathay by Little Langdale and Collath and Skelleth. It was a warm mild morning with threatening of rain. The vale of Little Langdale looked bare and unlovely. Collath was wild and interesting, from the peat carts and peat gatherers — the valley all perfumed with the gale and wild thyme. The woods about the waterfall veined with rich yellow Broom. A succession of delicious views from Skelleth to Brathay. We met near Skelleth a pretty little boy with a wallet over his shoulder. He came from Hawkshead and was going to "late a lock"[2] of meal. He spoke gently and without complaint. When I asked him if he got enough to eat,

[2]. Beg a measure of (dialect).

'I saw wild roses in the hedges.'

he looked surprized, and said "Nay". He was 7 years old but seemed not more than 5. We drank tea at Mr. Ibbetson's, and returned by Ambleside. Lent 3 : 9 : 0 to the potter at Kendal. Met John on our return home at about 10 o'clock. Saw a primrose in blossom.

[*June 17th,*] *Tuesday.* We put the new window in. I ironed, and worked about a good deal in house and garden. In the evening we walked for letters. Found one for Coleridge at Rydale, and I returned much tired.

[*June 18th,*] *Wednesday.* We walked round the lake in the morning and in the evening to the lower waterfall at Rydale. It was a warm dark, lowering evening.

[*June 19th,*] *Thursday.* A very hot morning. W. and I walked up to Mr. Simpson's. W. and old Mr. S. went to fish in Wytheburn water. I dined with John and lay under the trees. The afternoon changed from clear to cloudy, and to clear again. John and I walked up to the waterfall, and to Mr. Simpson's; and with Miss Simpson met the fishers. W. caught a pike weighing 4¾ lbs. There was a gloom almost terrible over Grasmere water and vale. A few drops fell but not much rain. No Coleridge, whom we fully expected.

[*June 20th,*] *Friday.* I worked in the garden in the morning. Wm. prepared pea sticks. Threatening for rain, but yet it comes not. On Wednesday evening a poor man called, a potter — he had been long ill, but was now recovered, and his wife was lying in of her 4th child. The parish would not help him, because he had implements of trade, etc. etc. We gave him 6d.

[*June 21st,*] *Saturday.* In the morning W. and I went to Ambleside to get his tooth drawn, and put in. A fine clear morning but cold. W.'s tooth drawn with very little pain — he slept till 3 o'clock. Young Mr. S. drank tea and supped with us. They fished in Rydale water and they caught 2 small fishes — W. no bite —

John 3. Miss Simpson and 3 children called — I walked with them to Rydale. The evening cold and clear and frosty but the wind was falling as I returned — I staid at home about an hour and then walked up the hill to Rydale lake. Grasmere looked so beautiful that my heart was almost melted away. It was quite calm, only spotted with sparkles of light. The church visible. On our return all distant objects had faded away — all but the hills. The reflection of the light bright sky above Black Quarter was very solemn. Mr. S. did not go till 12 o'clock.

[*June 22nd,*] *Sunday*. In the morning W. and I walked towards Rydale and up into the wood but finding it not very pleasant we returned — sauntered in the garden — a showery day. In the evening I planted a honeysuckle round the yew tree. In the evening we walked for letters — no letters. No news of Coleridge. Jimmy Benson came home drunk beside us.

[*June 23rd,*] *Monday*. Mr. Simpson called in the morning. Tommy's Father dead.W. and I went into Langdale to fish. The morning was very cold. I sate at the foot of the lake, till my head ached with cold. The view exquisitely beautiful, through a gate, and under a sycamore tree beside the first house going into Loughrigg. Elter-water looked barren, and the view from the church less beautiful than in winter. When W. went down to the water to fish, I lay under the [? wind], my head pillowed upon a mossy rock, and slept about 10 minutes, which relieved my headach. We ate our dinner together, and parted again. Wm. was afraid he had lost his line and sought me. An old man saw me just after I had crossed the stepping stones and was going through a copse — "Ho, wherever were you going?" "To Elterwater Bridge" — "Why", says he, "it's well I saw you; ye were gane to Little Langdale by Wrynose", and several other places which he ran over with a mixture of triumph, good-nature and wit — "It's well I saw

Windermere, by William Havell

Picnic on Lake Windermere, by John Harden

you or you'd ha' been lost." The [? evening] grew very pleasant — We sate on the side of the hill looking to Elterwater. I was much tired and returned home to tea. W. went to fish for pike in Rydale. John came in when I had done tea, and he and I carried a jug of tea to William. We met him in the old road from Rydale. He drank his tea upon the turf. The setting sun threw a red purple light upon the rocks, and stone walls of Rydale, which gave them a most interesting and beautiful appearance.

[*June 24th,*] *Tuesday*. W. went to Ambleside. John walked out. I made tarts, etc. Mr. B. Simpson called and asked us to tea. I went to the view of Rydale, to meet William. John went to him — I returned. W. and I drank tea at Mr. Simpson's. Brought down lemon-thyme, greens, etc. The old woman was very happy to see us, and we were so in the pleasure we gave. She was an affecting picture of patient disappointment, suffering under no particular affliction.

[*June 25th,*] *Wednesday*. A very rainy day. I made a shoe. Wm. and John went to fish in Langdale in the evening. I went above the house, and gathered flowers, which I planted, foxgloves, etc. On Sunday Mr. and Mrs. Coleridge and Hartley came. The day was very warm. We sailed to the foot of Loughrigg. They staid with us three weeks, and till the Thursday following, *i.e.* till the 23rd of July. On the Friday preceding their departure we drank tea at the island. The weather very delightful, and on the Sunday we made a great fire, and drank tea in Bainriggs with the Simpsons. I accompanied Mrs. C. to Wytheburne, and returned with W. to tea at Mr. Simpson's. It was excessively hot, but the day after, Friday 24th

July, still hotter. All the morning I was engaged in unpacking our Somersetshire goods and in making pies. The house was a hot oven, but yet we could not bake the pies. I was so weary, I could not walk: so I went and sate with Wm. in the orchard. We had a delightful half-hour in the warm still evening.

THE RAVEN.

[*July*] *26th, Saturday.* Still hotter. I sate with W. in the orchard all the morning, and made my shoes. In the afternoon from excessive heat I was ill in the headach and toothach and went to bed — I was refreshed with washing myself after I got up, but it was too hot to walk till near dark, and then I sate upon the wall finishing my shoes.

[*July*] *27th, Sunday.* Very warm. Molly ill. John bathed in the lake. I wrote out *Ruth* in the afternoon. In the morning, I read Mr. Knight's *Landscape.* After tea we rowed down to Loughrigg Fell, visited the white foxglove, gathered wild strawberries, and walked up to view Rydale. We lay a long time looking at the lake; the shores all embrowned with the scorching sun. The ferns were turning yellow, that is, here and there one was quite turned. We walked round by Benson's wood home. The lake was now most still, and reflected the beautiful yellow and blue and purple and grey colours of the sky. We heard a strange sound in the Bainriggs wood, as we were floating on the water; it *seemed* in the wood, but it must have been above it, for presently we saw a raven very high above us. It called out, and the dome of the sky seemed to echo the sound. It called again and again as it flew onwards, and the mountains gave back the sound, seeming as if from their center; a musical bell-like answering to the bird's hoarse voice. We heard both the call of the bird, and the echo, after we could see him no longer. We walked up to the top of the hill again in view of Rydale — met Mr. and Miss Simpson on horseback. The crescent moon which had shone upon the water was now gone down. Returned to supper at 10 o'clock.

[*July 28th,*] *Monday Morning.* Received a letter from Coleridge enclosing one from Mr. Davy about the *Lyrical Ballads.* Intensely hot. I made pies in the morning. William went into the wood, and altered his poems. In the evening it was so very warm that I was too much tired to walk.

[*July 29th,*] *Tuesday.* Still very hot. We gathered peas for dinner. We walked up in the evening to find out Hewetson's cottage but it was too dark. I was sick and weary.

[*July 30th,*] *Wednesday.* Gathered peas for Mrs. Simpson — John and I walked up with them — very hot — Wm. had intended going to Keswick. I was obliged to lie down after dinner from excessive heat and headach. The evening excessively beautiful — a rich reflection of the moon, the moonlight, clouds and the hills, and from the Rays gap a huge rainbow pillar. We sailed upon the lake till it was 10 o'clock.

[*July 31st,*] *Thursday.* All the morning I was busy copying poems. Gathered peas, and in the afternoon Coleridge came, very hot; he brought the 2nd volume of the Anthology. The men went to bathe, and we afterwards sailed down to Loughrigg. Read poems on the water, and let the boat take its own course. We walked a long time upon Loughrigg. I returned in the grey twilight. The moon just setting as we reached home.

August 1st, Friday. In the morning I copied *The Brothers.* Coleridge and Wm. went down to the lake. They returned, and we all went together to Mary Point, where we sate in the breeze and the shade, and read Wm.'s poems. Altered *The Whirlblast,* etc. Mr. Simpson came to tea and Mr. B. Simpson afterwards. We drank tea in the orchard.

[*August*] *2nd, Saturday Morning.* Wm. and Coleridge went to Keswick. John went with them to Wytheburn, and staid all day fishing, and brought home 2 small pikes at night. I accompanied them to Lewthwaite's cottage, and on my return papered Wm.'s room, I afterwards lay down till tea time and after tea worked at my shifts in the orchard. A grey evening. About 8 o'clock it gathered for rain, and I had the scatterings of a shower, but afterwards the lake became of a glassy calmness, and all was still. I sate till I could see no longer, and then continued my work in the house.

[*August*] *3rd, Sunday Morning.* I made pies and stuffed the pike — baked a loaf. Headach after dinner — I lay down. A letter from Wm. roused me, desiring us to go to Keswick. After writing to Wm. we walked as far as Mrs. Simpson's and ate black cherries. A heavenly warm evening, with scattered clouds upon the hills. There was a vernal greenness upon the grass, from the rains of the morning and

Keswick Lake from the East Side, by William Westall

afternoon. Peas for dinner.

[*August*] 4*th, Monday.* Rain in the night. I tied up scarlet beans, nailed the honeysuckles, etc. etc. John was prepared to walk to Keswick all the morning. He seized a returned chaise and went after dinner. I pulled a large basket of peas and sent to Keswick by a returned chaise. A very cold evening. Assisted to spread out linen in the morning.

[*August*] 5*th, Tuesday.* Dried the linen in the morning. The air still cold. I pulled a bag full of peas for Mrs. Simpson. Miss Simpson drank tea with me, and supped, on her return from Ambleside. A very fine evening. I sate on the wall making my shifts till I could see no longer. Walked half-way home with Miss Simpson.

August 6th, Wednesday. A rainy morning. I ironed till dinner time — sewed till near dark — then pulled a basket of peas, and afterwards boiled and picked gooseberries. William came home from Keswick at 11 o'clock. A very fine night.

August 7th, Thursday Morning. Packed up the mattrass and sent to Keswick. Boiled gooseberries — N.B. 2 lbs. of sugar in the first panfull, 3 quarts all good measure — 3 lbs. in the 2nd 4 quarts — 2½ lbs. in the 3rd. A very fine day. William composing in the wood in the morning. In the evening we walked to Mary Point. A very fine sunset.

[*August 8th,*] *Friday Morning.* We intended going to Keswick, but were pre-vented by the excessive heat. Nailed up scarlet beans in the morning. Drank tea at

Mr. Simpson's, and walked over the mountains by Wattendlath. Very fine gooseberries at Mr. S.'s. A most enchanting walk. Wattendlath a heavenly scene. Reached Coleridge's at eleven o'clock.

[*August 9th,*] *Saturday Morning.* I walked with Coleridge in the Windy Brow woods.

[*August 10th,*] *Sunday.* Very hot. The C.'s went to church. We sailed upon Derwent in the evening.

[*August 11th,*] *Monday Afternoon.* Walked with C. to Windy Brow.

[*August 12th,*] *Tuesday.* Drank tea with the Cockins — Wm. and I walked along the Cockermouth road. He was altering his poems.

[*August 13th,*] *Wednesday.* Made the Windy Brow seat.

[*August 14th,*] *Thursday Morning.* Called at the Speddings. In the evening walked in the wood with W. Very very beautiful the moon.

[*August 15th.*] Friday morning W. in the wood — I went with Hartley to see the Cockins and to buy bacon. In the evening we walked to Water End — feasted on gooseberries at Silver Hill.

[*August 16th.*] Saturday morning worked for Mrs. C. — walked with Coleridge intending to gather raspberries — joined by Miss Spedding.

August 17th, Sunday. Came home. Dined in Borrowdale. A rainy morning, but a fine evening — saw the Bristol prison and Bassenthwaite at the same time — Wm. read us *The Seven Sisters* on a stone.

[*August 18th,*] *Monday.* Putting linen by and mending — walked with John to Mr. Simpson's and met Wm. in returning. A fine warm day.

[*August 19th,*] *Tuesday.* Mr. and Miss Simpson dined with us — Miss S. and Brother drank tea in the orchard.

[*August 20th,*] *Wednesday.* I worked in the morning. Cold in the evening and rainy. Did not walk.

[*August 21st,*] *Thursday.* Read *Wallenstein* and sent it off — worked in the morning — walked with John round the two lakes — gathered white fox-glove seeds and found Wm. in Bainriggs at our return.

[*August*] 22*nd, Friday.* Very cold. Baking in the morning, gathered pea seeds and took up — lighted a fire upstairs. Walked as far as Rydale with John intending to have gone on to Ambleside, but we found the papers at Rydale — Wm. walking in the wood all the time. John and he went out after our return — I mended stockings. Wind very high shaking the corn.

[*August*] 23*rd, Saturday.* A very fine morning. Wm. was composing all the morning. I shelled peas, gathered beans, and worked in the garden till ½ past 12. Then walked with Wm. in the wood. The gleams of sunshine, and the stirring trees, and gleaming boughs, chearful lake, most delightful. After dinner we walked to Ambleside — showery — went to see Mr. Partridge's house. Came home by Clappersgate. We had intended going by Rydale woods, but it was cold — I was not well, and tired. Got tea immediately and had a fire. Did not reach home till 7 o'clock — mended stockings and Wm. read *Peter Bell.* He read us the poem of *Joanna,* beside the Rothay by the roadside.

Rossthwaite, Borrowdale, by Thomas Austin

[*August*] 24*th, Sunday*. A fine cool pleasant breezy day — walked in the wood in the morning. Mr. Twining called. John walked up to Mr. Simpson's in the evening — I staid at home and wrote to Mrs. Rawson and my aunt Cookson — I was ill in the afternoon and lay down — got up restored by a sound sleep.

[*August* 25*th*,] *Monday*. A fine day — walked in the wood in the morning and to the firgrove — walked up to Mr. Simpson's in the evening.

[*August*] 26*th, Tuesday*. We walked in the evening to Ambleside — Wm. not quite well. I bought sacking for the mattrass. A very fine solemn evening. The wind blew very free from the islands at Rydale. We went on the other side of Rydale, and sate a long time looking at the mountains, which were all black at Grasmere, and very bright in Rydale; Grasmere exceedingly dark, and Rydale of a light yellow green.

[*August*] 27*th, Wednesday*. In the morning Wm. walked [?]. We walked along the shore of the lake in the evening, went over into Langdale and down to Loughrigg Tarn — a very fine evening calm and still.

[*August* 28*th*,] *Thursday*. Still very fine weather. I baked bread and cakes. In the evening we walked round the Lake by Rydale. Mr. Simpson came to fish.

[*August* 29*th*,] *Friday Evening*. We walked to Rydale to inquire for letters. We walked over the hill by the firgrove. I sate upon a rock, and observed a flight of swallows gathering together high above my head. They flew towards Rydale. We walked through the wood over the stepping-stones. The lake of Rydale very beautiful, partly still. John and I left Wm. to compose an inscription — that about the path. We had a very fine walk by the gloomy lake. There was a curious yellow reflection in the water, as of corn fields. There was no light in the clouds from which it appeared to come.

August 30th, Saturday Morning. I was baking bread, pies and dinner. It was very warm. William finished his Inscription of the Pathway, then walked in the wood; and when John returned, he sought him, and they bathed together. I read a little of Boswell's *Life of Johnson*. I had a headach and went to lie down in the orchard. I was roused by a shout that Anthony Harrison was come. We sate in the orchard till tea time. Drank tea early, and rowed down the lake which was stirred by breezes. We looked at Rydale, which was soft, chearful, and beautiful. We then went to peep into Langdale. The Pikes were very grand. We walked back to the view of Rydale, which was now a dark mirror. We rowed home over a lake still as glass, and then went to George Mackareth's to hire a horse for John. A fine moonlight night. The beauty of the moon was startling, as it rose to us over Loughrigg Fell. We returned to our supper at 10 o'clock. Thomas Ashburner brought us our 8th cart of coals since May 17th.

[*August*] 31*st, Sunday.* Anthony Harrison and John left us at ½ past seven — a very fine morning. A great deal of corn is cut in the vale, and the whole prospect, thought not tinged with a general autumnal yellow, yet softened down into a mellowness of colouring, which seems to impart softness to the forms of hills and mountains. At 11 o'clock Coleridge came, when I was walking in the still clear moonshine in the garden. He came over Helvellyn. Wm. was gone to bed, and John also, worn out with his ride round Coniston. We sate and chatted till ½-past three, W. in his dressing gown. Coleridge read us a part of *Christabel*. Talked much about the mountains, etc. etc. Miss Thrale's [?] — Losh's opinion of Southey — the first of poets.

September 1st, Monday Morning. We walked in the wood by the lake. W. read *Joanna,* and the *Firgrove,* to Coleridge. They bathed. The morning was delightful, with somewhat of an autumnal freshness. After dinner, Coleridge discovered a rock-seat in the orchard. Cleared away the brambles. Coleridge obliged to go to bed after tea. John and I followed Wm. up the hill, and then returned to go to Mr. Simpson's. We borrowed some bottles for bottling rum. The evening somewhat frosty and grey, but very pleasant. I broiled Coleridge a mutton chop, which he ate in bed. Wm. was gone to bed. I chatted with John and Coleridge till near 12.

[*September*] 2*nd, Tuesday.* In the morning they all went to Stickle Tarn. A very fine, warm, sunny, beautiful morning. I baked a pie etc. for dinner — Little Sally was with me. The fair-day. Miss Simpson and Mr. came down to tea — we walked to the fair. There seemed very few people and very few stalls, yet I believe there were many cakes and much beer sold. My brothers came home to dinner at 6 o'clock. We drank tea immediately after by candlelight. It was a lovely moonlight night. We talked much about a house on Helvellyn. The moonlight shone only upon the village. It did not eclipse the village lights, and the sound of dancing and merriment came along the still air. I walked with Coleridge and Wm. up the lane and by the church, and then lingered with Coleridge in the garden.

Borrowdale, with Children Playing on the Banks of a Brook, by William Collins

John and Wm. were both gone to bed, and all the lights out.

September 3rd, Wednesday. Coleridge, Wm., and John went from home, to go upon Helvellyn with Mr. Simpson. They set out after breakfast. I accompanied them up near the blacksmith's. A fine coolish morning. I ironed till ½ past 3 — now very hot — I then went to a funeral at John Dawson's. About 10 men and 4 women. Bread, cheese, and ale. They talked sensibly and chearfully about common things. The dead person, 56 years of age, buried by the parish. The coffin was neatly lettered and painted black, and covered with a decent cloth. They set the corpse down at the door; and, while we stood within the threshold, the men with their hats off sang with decent and solemn countenances a verse of a funeral psalm. The corpse was then borne down the hill, and they sang till they had passed the Town-End. I was affected to tears while we stood in the house, the coffin lying before me. There were no near kindred, no children. When we got out of the dark house the sun was shining, and the prospect looked so divinely beautiful as I never saw it. It seemed more sacred than I had ever seen it, and yet more allied to human life. The green fields, neighbours of the churchyard, were as green as possible; and, with the brightness of the sunshine, looked quite gay. I thought she was going to a quiet spot, and I could not help weeping very much.

A Village Fair, by W. H. Pyne

When we came to the bridge, they began to sing again, and stopped during four lines before they entered the churchyard. The priest met us — he did not look as a man ought to do on such an occasion — I had seen him half-drunk the day before in a pot-house. Before we came with the corpse one of the company observed he wondered what sort of cue our Parson would be in! N.B. It was the day after the Fair. I had not finished ironing till 7 o'clock. The wind was now high and I did not walk — writing my journal now at 8 o'clock. Wm. and John came home at 10 o'clock.

September 4th, Thursday. A fine warm day. I was busy all the morning making a mattrass. Mr. Simpson called in the afternoon. Wm. walked in the wood in the morning, and in the evening as we set forward to walk — a letter from Mrs. Clarkson. We walked into the black quarter. The patches of corn very interesting.

[*September 5th,*] *Friday Morning*. Finished the mattrass, ironed the white bed in the afternoon — when I was putting it up Mr. and Mrs. Losh arrived while Wm. and John were walking.

[*September 6th,*] *Saturday Morning*. Breakfasted with the Loshes — very warm — returned through Rydale woods. The Clarksons dined. After tea we walked round Rydale — a little rain.

[*September*] *7th, Sunday Morning*. Rainy. Walked before dinner over the stepping-stones to Langdale and home on the other side of the lake. I lay down after dinner. Wm. poorly. Walked into the Black Quarter.

September 8th, Monday. Morning very rainy. The Clarksons left us after dinner — still rainy. We walked towards Rydale, and then to Mr. Olliff's gate — a fine evening.

[*September*] *9th, Tuesday Morning*. Mr. Marshall came — he dined with us. My Brothers walked with him round the lakes after dinner — windy — we went to the island. W. and I after to tea. John and I went to the B. quarter, before supper went to seek a horse at Dawson's, Firgrove. After supper, talked of Wm.'s poems.

Sept[ember] 10th, Wednesday. After breakfast Mr. Marshall, Wm. and John went on horseback to Keswick — I wrote to Mrs. Marshall — a fine autumn day. I had a fire. Paid Mr. Bonsfield 8 : 2 : 11. After tea walked with French Beans to Mr. Simpson's — went up to the Forest side above a deserted house — sat till twilight came on. Mr. and Miss S. came down with me and supped.

[*September*] *11th, Thursday*. All the morning mending white gown — washed my head — Molly washing. Drank tea at Mr. Simpson's. Found Wm. at home at my return — he was unable to go on with Mr. Marshall and parted from him in Borrowdale. Made tea after my return.

Sept[ember] 12th, Friday. I worked in the morning. Cut my thumb. Walked in the Firgrove before dinner — after dinner sate under the trees in the orchard — a rainy morning, but very fine afternoon. Miss Simpson called for my packing needle. The Fern of the mountains now spreads yellow veins among the trees; the coppice wood turns brown. William observed some affecting little things in Borrowdale. A decayed house with this inscription [*blank space in MS.*] in the

Laundry Maid outside a Cottage, by John Harden

Waterfall near Sourmilk Gill ('Churnmilk force'), Easedale, by Thomas Austin

Church yard, the tall silent rocks seen thro' the broken windows. A kind of rough column put upon the gavel end of a house, with a ball stone, smooth from the river placed upon it for ornament. Near it one stone like it upon an old mansion, carefully hewn.

September 13th, Saturday Morning. William writing his Preface — did not walk. Jones, and Mr. Palmer came to tea. We walked with them to Borricks — a lovely evening, but the air frosty — worked when I returned home. Wm. walked out. John came home from Mr. Marshall. Sent back word to Mrs. Clarkson.

[*September*] 14th, *Sunday Morning.* Made bread. A sore thumb from a cut. A lovely day. Read Boswell in the house in the morning, and after dinner under the bright yellow leaves of the orchard. The pear trees a bright yellow. The apple trees green still. A sweet lovely afternoon.

Here I have long neglected my Journal. John came home in the evening, after Jones left us. Jones returned again on the Friday, the 19th September. Jones stayed with us till Friday, 26th September. Coleridge came on Tuesday 23rd and went home with Jones. Charles Lloyd called on Tuesday, 23rd, and on Sunday 28th we drank tea and supped with him and on that day heard of the Abergavenny's arrival. While Jones was with us we had much rainy weather. On Sunday 21st Tom Myers and Father called, and on the 28th Mr. and Miss Smith.

[*September*] 29th, *on Monday.* John left us. Wm. and I parted with him in sight of

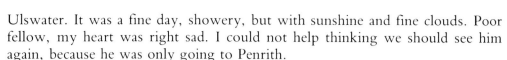

Ulswater. It was a fine day, showery, but with sunshine and fine clouds. Poor fellow, my heart was right sad. I could not help thinking we should see him again, because he was only going to Penrith.

September 30th, on Tuesday. Charles Lloyd dined with us. We walked homewards with him after dinner. It rained very hard. Rydale was extremely wild, and we had a fine walk. We sate quietly and comfortably by the fire. I wrote the last sheet of Notes and Preface. Went to bed at twelve o'clock.

October 1st, Wednesday. A fine morning, a showery night. The lake still in the morning; in the forenoon flashing light from the beams of the sun, as it was ruffled by the wind. We corrected the last sheet.

October 2nd, Thursday. A very rainy morning. We walked after dinner to observe the torrents. I followed Wm. to Rydale, he afterwards went to Butterlip How. I came home to receive the Lloyds. They walked with us to see Churnmilk force and the Black quarter. The Black Quarter looked marshy, and the general prospect was cold, but the Force was very grand. The Lichens are now coming out afresh, I carried home a collection in the afternoon. We had a pleasant conversation about the manners of the rich — avarice, inordinate desires, and the effeminacy, unnaturalness, and the unworthy objects of education. After the Lloyds were gone we walked — a showery evening. The moonlight lay upon the hills like snow.

October 3rd, Friday. Very rainy all morning. Little Sally learning to mark. Wm. walked to Ambleside after dinner, I went with him part of the way. He talked much about the object of his essay for the second volume of "L. B." I returned expecting the Simpsons — they did not come. I should have met Wm. but my teeth ached and it was showery and late — he returned after 10. Amos Cottle's death in the *Morning Post*. Wrote to S. Lowthian.

N.B. When William and I returned from accompanying Jones we met an old man almost double. He had on a coat, thrown over his shoulders, above his waistcoat and coat. Under this he carried a bundle, and had an apron on and a night-cap. His face was interesting. He had dark eyes and a long nose. John, who afterwards met him at Wytheburn, took him for a Jew. He was of Scotch parents, but had been born in the army. He had had a wife, and "a good woman, and it pleased God to bless us with ten children". All these were dead but one, of whom he had not heard for many years, a sailor. His trade was to gather leeches, but now leeches are scarce, and he had not strength for it. He lived by begging, and was making his way to Carlisle, where he should buy a few godly books to sell. He said leeches were very scarce partly owing to this dry season, but many years have been scarce — he supposed it owing to their being much sought after, that they did not breed fast, and were of slow growth. Leeches were formerly 2s. 6d. [per] 100; they are now 30s. He had been hurt in driving a cart, his leg broke, his body driven over, his skull fractured. He felt no pain till he recovered from his first insensibility. It was then late in the evening, when the light was just going away.

October 4th, 1800, Saturday. A very rainy, or rather showery and gusty, morn-

Ullswater with Goldrigg Bridge, by John Glover

ing; for often the sun shines. Thomas Ashburner could not go to Keswick. Read a part of Lamb's Play. The language is often very beautiful, but too imitative in particular phrases, words, etc. The characters, except Margaret's, unintelligible, and, except Margaret's, do not show themselves in action. Coleridge came in while we were at dinner, very wet — we talked till 12 o'clock. He had sate up all the night before, writing Essays for the newspaper. His youngest child had been very ill in convulsion fits. Exceedingly delighted with the second part of *Christabel*.

October 5th, Sunday Morning. Coleridge read a 2nd time *Christabel;* we had increasing pleasure. A delicious morning. Wm. and I were employed all the morning in writing an addition to the Preface. Wm. went to bed, very ill after working after dinner. Coleridge and I walked to Ambleside after dark with the letter. Returned to tea at 9 o'clock. Wm. still in bed, and very ill. Silver How in both lakes.

[*October 6th,*] *Monday.* A rainy day. Coleridge intending to go, but did not get off. We walked after dinner to Rydale. After tea read *The Pedlar.* Determined not to print *Christabel* with the L. B.

[*October 7th,*] *Tuesday.* Coleridge went off at eleven o'clock. I went as far as Mr. Simpson's. Returned with Mary. She drank tea here. I was very ill in the evening at the Simpsons — went to bed — supped there. Returned with Miss S. and Mrs. J. — heavy showers. Found Wm. at home. I was still weak and unwell — went to bed immediately.

[*October 8th,*] *Wednesday.* A threatening bad morning — We dried the linen. Frequent threatening of showers. Received a £5 note from Montagu. Wm. walked to Rydale. I copied a part of *The Beggar* in the morning. I was not quite

well in the evening, therefore I did not walk — Wm. walked. A very mild moonlight night. Glow-worms everywhere.

[*October 9th,*] *Thursday.* I was ironing all the day till tea time. Very rainy. Wm. and I walked in the evening, intending to go to Lloyd's, but it came on so very rainy that we were obliged to shelter at Fleming's. A grand Ball at Rydale. After sitting some time we went homewards and were again caught by a shower and sheltered under the sycamores at the boathouse — a very cold snowlike rain. A man called in a soldier's dress — he was thirty years old, of Cockermouth, had lost a leg and thigh in battle, was going to his home. He could earn more money in travelling with his ass than at home.

October 10th, Friday. In the morning when I arose the mists were hanging over the opposite hills, and the tops of the highest hills were covered with snow. There was a most lovely combination at the head of the vale of the yellow autumnal hills wrapped in sunshine, and overhung with partial mists, the green and yellow trees, and the distant snow-topped mountains. It was a most heavenly morning. The Cockermouth traveller came with thread, hardware, mustard, etc. She is very healthy; has travelled over the mountains these thirty years. She does not mind the storms, if she can keep her goods dry. Her husband will not travel with an ass, because it is the tramper's badge; she would have one to relieve her from the weary load. She was going to Ulverston, and was to return to Ambleside Fair. After I had finished baking I went out with Wm., Mrs Jameson and Miss Simpson towards Rydale — the fern among the rocks exquisitely beautiful. We turned home and walked to Mr. Gell's. After dinner Wm. went to bed — I read Southey's letter. Miss Simpson and Mrs. Jameson came to tea. After tea we went to Lloyd's — a fine evening as we went, but rained in returning — we were wet

— found them not at home. I wrote to Mrs. Clarkson. Sent off *The Beggar,* etc., by Thomas Ashburner who went to fetch our 9th cart of coals. William sat up after me, writing *Point Rash Judgment.*

[*October*] 11*th, Saturday.* A fine October morning. Sat in the house working all the morning. William composing. Sally Ashburner learning to mark. After dinner we walked up Greenhead Gill in search of a sheepfold. We went by Mr. Olliff's, and through his woods. It was a delightful day, and the views looked excessively chearful and beautiful, chiefly that from Mr. Olliff's field, where our house is to be built. The colours of the mountains soft and rich, with orange fern; the cattle pasturing upon the hill-tops; kites sailing in the sky above our heads; sheep bleating and in lines and chains and patterns scattered over the mountains. They come down and feed on the little green islands in the beds of the torrents, and so may be swept away. The sheepfold is falling away. It is built nearly in the form of a heart unequally divided. Look down the brook, and see the drops rise upwards and sparkle in the air at the little falls, the higher sparkles the tallest. We walked along the turf of the mountain till we came to a cattle track, made by the cattle which come upon the hills. We drank tea at Mr. Simpson's, returned at about nine — a fine mild night.

October 12th, Sunday. Beautiful day. Sate in the house writing in the morning while Wm. went into the wood to compose. Wrote to John in the morning, copied poems for the L. B.; in the evening wrote to Mrs. Rawson. Mary Jameson and Sally Ashburner dined. We pulled apples after dinner, a large basket full. We walked before tea by Bainriggs to observe the many-coloured foliage. The oaks dark green with yellow leaves, the birches generally still green, some near the water yellowish, the sycamore crimson and crimson-tufted, the mountain ash a deep orange, the common ash lemon-colour, but many ashes still fresh in their summer green. Those that were discoloured chiefly near the water. William composing in the evening. Went to bed at 12 o'clock.

October 13th, Monday. A grey day. Mists on the hills. We did not walk in the morning. I copied poems on the Naming of Places. A fair at Ambleside. Walked in the Black Quarter at night.

[*October*] 14*th, Tuesday.* Wm. lay down after dinner — I read Southey's Spain. The wind rose very high at evening. Wm. walked out just at bedtime — I went to bed early. We walked before dinner to Rydale.

[*October 15th,*] *Wednesday.* A very fine clear morning. After Wm. had composed a little, I persuaded him to go into the orchard. We walked backwards and forwards. The prospect most divinely beautiful from the seat; all colours, all melting into each other. I went in to put bread in the oven, and we both walked within view of Rydale. Wm. again composed at the sheep-fold after dinner. I walked with him to Wytheburn, and he went on to Keswick. I drank tea, and supped at Mr. Simpson's. A very cold frosty air and a spangled sky in returning. Mr. and Miss S. came with me. Wytheburn looked very wintry, but yet there was a foxglove blossoming by the roadside.

October 16th, Thursday. A very fine morning — starched and hung out linen — a

'. . . but yet there was a foxglove blossoming by the roadside.'

very fine day. John Fisher, F. A., and S. A. and Molly working in the garden. Wrote to Miss Nicholson. I walked as far as Rydale between 3 and 4 — Ironed till six — got tea and wrote to Mr. Griffith. A letter from Mr. Clarkson.

[*October*] 17*th, Friday.* A very fine grey morning. The swan hunt. Sally working in the garden. I walked round the lake between ¼ past 12 and ½ past one. Wrote to M. H. After dinner walked to Lloyd's — carried my letters to Miss N. and M. H. The Lloyds not in — I waited for them — Charles not well. Letters from M. H., Biggs and John. In my walk in the morning, I observed Benson's honeysuckles in flower, and great beauty. It was a very fine mild evening. Ll.'s servants came with me to Parke's. I found Wm. at home, where he had been almost ever since my departure. Coleridge had done nothing for the L. B. Working hard for Stuart. Glow-worms in abundance.

[*October* 18*th,*] *Saturday.* A very fine October morning. William worked all the morning at the sheepfold, but in vain. He lay down in the afternoon till 7 o'clock, but could not sleep. I slept, my head better — he unable to work. We did not walk all day.

[*October* 19*th,*] *Sunday Morning.* We rose late, and walked directly after breakfast. The tops of G[ras]mere mountains cut off. Rydale was very, very beautiful. The surface of the water quite still, like a dim mirror. The colours of the large island exquisitely beautiful, and the trees still fresh and green were magnified by the mists. The prospects on the west side of the Lake were very beautiful. We sate at the "two points" looking up to Park's. The lowing of the cattle was echoed by a hollow voice in Knab Scar. We went upon Loughrigg Fell and were disappointed with G[ras]mere — It did not look near so beautiful as Rydale. We returned home over the stepping-stones. Wm. got to work. We are not to dine till 4 o'clock.— Dined at ½ past 5 — Mr. Simpson dined and drank tea with us. We went to bed immediately after he left us.

[*October*] 20*th, Monday*. William worked in the morning at the sheepfold. After dinner we walked to Rydale, crossed the stepping-stones, and while we were walking under the tall oak trees the Lloyds called out to us. They went with us on the western side of Rydale. The lights were very grand upon the woody Rydale hills. Those behind dark and topp'd with clouds. The two lakes were divinely beautiful. Grasmere excessively solemn and the whole lake was calm, and dappled with soft grey ripples. The Lloyds staid with us till 8 o'clock. We then walked to the top of the hill at Rydale. Very mild and warm. About 6 glow-worms shining faintly. We went up as far as the grove. When we came home the fire was out. We ate our supper in the dark, and went to bed immediately. William was disturbed in the night by the rain coming into his room, for it was a very rainy night. The ash leaves lay across the road.

[*October*] 21*st, Tuesday*. We walked in the morning past Mr. Gell's — a very fine clear sharp sunny morning. We drank tea at the Lloyds. It was very cold in the evening, quite frosty and starlight. Wm. had been unsuccessful in the morning at the sheepfold. The reflection of the ash scattered, and the tree stripped.

[*October 22nd,*] *Wednesday Morning.* We walked to Mr. Gell's — a very fine morning. Wm. composed without much success at the sheepfold. Coleridge came in to dinner. He had done nothing. We were very merry. C. and I went to look at the prospect from his seat. In the evening Stoddart came in when we were at tea, and after tea Mr. and Miss Simpson with with large potatoes and plumbs. Wm. read after supper, *Ruth,* etc.; Coleridge *Christabel.*

[*October*] 23rd, *Thursday.* Coleridge and Stoddart went to Keswick. We accompanied them to Wytheburn — a wintry grey morning from the top of the Raise. Grasmere looked like winter, and Wytheburn still more so. We called upon Mrs. Simpson and sate 10 minutes in returning. Wm. was not successful in composition in the evening.

[*October*] 24th, *Friday.* A very fine morning. We walked before Wm. began to work to the top of the Rydale hill. He was afterwards only partly successful in composition. After dinner we walked round Rydale lake, rich, calm, streaked, very beautiful. We went to the top of Loughrigg. Grasmere sadly inferior. We were much tired — Wm. went to bed till ½ past seven. The ash in our garden green, one close to it bare, the next nearly so.

[*October 25th,*] *Saturday.* A very rainy day. Wm. again unsuccessful. We could not walk, it was so very rainy. We read Rogers, Miss Seward, Cowper, etc.

[*October 26th,*] *Sunday.* Heavy rain all night, a fine morning after 10 o'clock. Wm. composed a good deal in the morning. The Lloyds came to dinner and were caught in a shower. Wm. read some of his poems after dinner. A terrible night. I went with Mrs. Lloyd to Newton's to see for lodgings. Mr. Simpson in coming from Ambleside called in for a glass of rum just before we went to bed.

Grasmere, by J. C. Ibbetson

October 27th, Monday. Not a rainy morning. The Hill tops covered with snow. Charles Lloyd came for his wife's glass. I walked home with him past Rydale. When he came I met him as I was carrying some cold meat to Wm. in the Fir-grove, I had before walked with him there for some time. It was a fine shelter from the wind. The coppices now nearly of one brown. An oak tree in a sheltered place near John Fisher's, not having lost any of its leaves, was quite brown and dry. We did not walk till after dinner. It was a fine wild moonlight night. Wm. could not compose much, fatigued himself with altering.

[*October*] *28th, Tuesday.* A very rainy night. I was baking bread in the morning and made a giblet pie. We walked out before dinner to our favourite field. The mists sailed along the mountains, and rested upon them, enclosing the whole vale. In the evening the Lloyds came. We drank tea with them at Borwick's and played a rubber at whist — stayed supper. Wm. looked very well — A fine moonlight night when we came home.

[*October 29th,*] *Wednesday.* William working at his poem all the morning. After dinner, Mr. Clarkson called. We went down to Borwick's and he and the Lloyds and Priscilla came back to drink tea with us. We met Stoddart upon the bridge. Played at cards. The Lloyds etc. went home to supper — Mr. Clarkson slept here.

[*October 30th,*] *Thursday.* A rainy morning. Mr. C. went over Kirkstone. Wm. talked all day, and almost all night, with Stoddart. Mrs. and Miss Ll. called in the morning. I walked with them to Tail End, a fine pleasant morning, but a very rainy afternoon. W. and I in the house all day.

[*October 31st,*] *Friday.* W. and I did not rise till 1 o'clock. W. very sick and very ill. S. and I drank tea at Lloyds and came home immediately after. A very fine moonlight night — The moon shone like herrings in the water.

[*November 1st,*] *Saturday.* William better. We met as we walked to Rydale a boy from Lloyd's, coming for *Don Quixote.* Talk in the evening. Tom Ashburner brought his 10th cart of coals.

[*November 2nd,*] *Sunday Morning.* We walked into the Black Quarter — a very fine morning — a succession of beautiful views, mists, etc. etc., much rain in the night. In the evening drank tea at Lloyds — found them all ill, in colds — came home to supper.

[*November 3rd,*] *Monday Morning.* Walked to Rydale — a cold day. Wm. and Stoddart still talking. Frequent showers in our walk. In the evening we talked merrily over the fire. The Speddings stopped at the door.

[*November 4th,*] *Tuesday.* Stoddart left us — I walked a little way with W. and

him. W. went to the Tarn, afterwards to the top of Seat Sandal. He was obliged to lie down in the tremendous wind. The snow blew from Helvellyn horizontally like smoke — the spray of the unseen waterfall like smoke. Miss Lloyd called upon me — I walked with her past Rydale. Wm. sadly tired — threatenings of the piles.

[*November 5th,*] *Wednesday.* Wm. not well. A very fine clear beautiful winter's day. I walked after dinner to Lloyd's — drank tea and Mrs. and Miss Lloyd came to Rydale with me. The moon was rising but the sky all over cloud. I made tea for William.

November 6th, Thursday. A very rainy morning and night. I was baking bread, dinner, and parkins. Charles and P. Lloyd called. Wm. somewhat better. Read *Point Rash Judgment.* The lake calm and very beautiful — a very rainy afternoon and night.

November 7th, Friday. A cold rainy morning. Wm. still unwell. I working and reading *Amelia.* The Michaelmas daisy droops, the pansies are full of flowers, the ashes opposite are green all but one, but they have lost many of their leaves. The copses are quite brown. The poor woman and child from Whitehaven drank tea — nothing warm that day. A very rainy morning. It cleared up in the afternoon. We expected the Lloyds but they did not come. Wm. still unwell. A rainy night.

November 8th, Saturday. A rainy morning. A whirlwind came that tossed about the leaves, and tore off the still green leaves of the ashes. A fine afternoon — Wm. and I walked out at 4 o'clock. Went as far as Rothay Bridge. Met the Butcher's man with a l[ette]r from Monk Lewis. The country very wintry — some oaks quite bare — others more sheltered with a few green leaves — others with brown leaves, but the whole face of the country in a winter covering. We went early to bed.

[*November 9th,*] *Sunday*. Wm. slept tolerably — better this morning. It was a frosty night. We walked to Rydale after dinner, partly expecting to meet the Lloyds. Mr. Simpson brought newspapers but met Molly with them. W. [?burnt] the sheepfold. A rainy night.

[*November 10th,*] *Monday*. I baked bread. A fine clear frosty morning. We walked after dinner to Rydale village. Jupiter over the hilltops, the only star, like a sun, flashed out at intervals from behind a black cloud.

[*November 11th,*] *Tuesday Morning*. Walked to Rydale before dinner for letters. William had been working at the sheepfold. They were salving sheep. A rainy morning. The Lloyds drank tea with us. Played at cards — Priscilla not well. We walked after they left us to the top of the Rydale hill — then towards Mr. Olliff's and towards the village. A mild night, partly cloudy, partly starlight. The cottage lights, the mountains not very distinct.

[*November 12th,*] *Wednesday*. We sate in the house all the day. Mr. Simpson called and found us at dinner — a rainy evening — he staid the evening and

Group Playing Cards, by John Harden

Lake Keswick, by J. M. W. Turner

supper. I lay down after dinner with a headach.

[*November 13th,*] *Thursday.* A stormy night. We sate in the house all the morning. Rainy weather. Old Mr. Simpson, Mrs. J. and Miss S. drank tea and supped, played at cards, found us at dinner. A poor woman from Hawkshead begged, a widow of Grasmere. A merry African from Longtown.

[*November 14th,*] *Friday.* I had a bad headach. Much wind, but a sweet mild morning. I nailed up trees. Sent Molly Ashburner to excuse us to Lloyds. Two letters from Coleridge, very ill. One from Sara H. One from S. Lowthian — I wrote to S. Hutchinson and received £3 from her.

[*November 15th,*] *Saturday Morning.* A terrible rain, so William prevented from going to Coleridge's. The afternoon fine and mild — I walked to the top of the hill for a headach. We both set forward at five o'clock after tea. A fine wild but not cold night. I walked with W. over the Raise. It was starlight. I parted with him very sad, unwilling not to go on. The hills, and the stars, and the white waters, with their ever varying yet ceaseless sound, were very impressive. I supped at the Simpsons'. Mr. P. walked home with me.

November 16th, Sunday. A very fine warm sunny morning. A letter from Coleridge, and one from Stoddart. Coleridge better. My head aching very much — I sent to excuse myself to Lloyds — then walked to the Cottage beyond Mr. Gell's. One beautiful ash tree sheltered, with yellow leaves, one low one quite green. Some low ashes green. A noise of boys in the rocks hunting some animal.

Walked a little in the garden when I came home — very pleasant. Now rain came on. Mr. Jackson called in the evening when I was at tea, brought me a letter from C. and W. C. better.

[*November 17th,*] *Monday Morning.* A fine clear frosty morning with a sharp wind. I walked to Keswick. Set off at 5 minutes past 10, and arrived at ½ past 2. I found them all well.

On *Tuesday* morning W. and C. set off towards Penrith. Wm. met Sara Hutchinson at Threlkeld. They arrived at Keswick at tea time.

[*November 19th,*] *Wednesday.* We walked by the lake side and they went to Mr. Denton's. I called upon the Miss Cockyns.

[*November 20th,*] *Thursday.* We spent the morning in the town. Mr. Jackson and Mr. Peach dined with us.

[*November 21st,*] *Friday.* A very fine day. Went to Mrs. Greaves'. Mrs. C. and I called upon the Speddings. A beautiful crescent moon.

[*November 22nd,*] *Saturday Morning.* After visiting Mr Peach's Chinese pictures we set off to Grasmere. A threatening and rather rainy morning. Arrived at G. very dirty and a little wet at the closing in of Evening. Wm. not quite well.

[*November 23rd,*] *Sunday.* Wm. not well. I baked bread and pie for dinner. Sara and I walked after dinner and met Mr. Gawthorpe, paid his bill and he drank tea with us — paid £5 for Mr. Bonsfield.

[*November 24th,*] *Monday.* A fine morning. Sara and I walked to Rydale. After dinner we went to Lloyd's, and drank tea, and supped. A sharp cold night, with sleet and snow. I had the tooth ach in the night. Took laudanum.

[*November 25th,*] *Tuesday.* Very ill — in bed all day — better in the evening — read *Tom Jones* — very sleepy — slept all night.

[*November 26th,*] *Wednesday.* Well in the morning. Wm. very well. We had a delightful walk up into Easedale. The tops of the mountains covered with snow, frosty and sunny, the roads slippery. A letter from Mary. The Lloyds drank tea. We walked with them near to Ambleside. A beautiful moonlight night. Sara and I walked before [? home]. William very well, and highly poetical.

November 27th, Thursday. Wrote to Tom Hutchinson to desire him to bring Mary with him from Stockton. A thaw, and the ground covered with snow. Sara and I walked before dinner.

[*November 28th,*] *Friday.* Coleridge walked over. Miss Simpson drank tea with us. William walked home with her. Coleridge was very unwell. He went to bed before Wm.'s return. Great boils upon his neck.

[*November 29th,*] *Saturday.* A fine day.

November 30th, Sunday. A very fine clear morning. Snow upon the ground everywhere. Sara and I walked towards Rydale by the upper road, and were obliged to return, because of the snow. Walked by moonlight.

[*December 1st,*] *Monday.* A thaw in the night, and the snow was entirely gone. Sara and I had a delightful walk by the upper Rydale road and Mr. King's. Coleridge unable to go home for his health. We walked by moonlight.

December 2nd, Tuesday. A rainy morning. Coleridge was obliged to set off. Sara and I met C. Lloyd and P. — turned back with them. I walked round the 2 lakes with Charles, very pleasant passing lights — I was sadly wet when we came home and very cold. Priscilla drank tea with us. We all walked to Ambleside. A pleasant moonlight evening, but not clear. Supped upon a hare. It came on a terrible evening. Hail, and wind, and cold, and rain.

December 3rd, Wednesday. We lay in bed till 11 o'clock. Wrote to John, and M. H. William and Sara and I walked to Rydale after tea — a very fine frosty night. Sara and W. walked round the other side. I was tired and returned home. We went to bed early.

[*December 4th,*] *Thursday.* Coleridge came in just as we finished dinner. Pork from the Simpsons. Sara and I walked round the 2 lakes — a very fine morning. C. ate nothing, to cure his boils. We walked after tea by moonlight to look at Langdale covered with snow, the Pikes not grand, but the Old Man very impressive. Cold and slippery, but exceedingly pleasant. Sat up till half-past one.

[*December 5th,*] *Friday Morning.* Terribly cold and rainy. Coleridge and Wm. set forwards towards Keswick, but the wind in Coleridge's eyes made him turn

back. Sara and I had a grand bread and cake baking. We were very merry in the evening, but grew sleepy soon, though we did not go to bed till twelve o'clock.

[*December 6th,*] *Saturday*. Wm. accompanied Coleridge to the foot of the Rays. A very pleasant morning. Sara and I accompanied him half-way to Keswick. Thirlemere was very beautiful even more so than in summer. William was not well, had laboured unsuccessfully. Charles Lloyd had called. Sara and I drank tea with Mrs. Simpson. A sharp shower met us — it rained a little when we came home — Mr. B. S. accompanied us. Miss S. at Ambleside. Wm. tired and not well. A letter from M. H.

[*December 7th,*] *Sunday*. A fine morning. I read. Sara wrote to Hartley, Wm. to Mary, I to Mrs. C. We walked just before dinner to the lakeside, and found out a seat in a tree. Windy, but pleasant. Sara and Wm. walked to the waterfalls at Rydale. I was unwell and went to bed till 8 o'clock — a pleasant mild evening — went to bed at 12. Miss Simpson called.

December 8th, Monday. A sweet mild morning. I wrote to Mrs. Cookson, and Miss Griffith.

[*December*] *9th, Tuesday*. I dined at Lloyd's. Wm. drank tea. Walked home. A pleasant starlight frosty evening. Reached home at one o'clock. Wm. finished his poem to-day.

[*December*] *10th, Wednesday*. Walked to Keswick. Snow upon the ground. A very fine day. Ate bread and ale at John Stanley's. Found Coleridge better. Stayed at Keswick till Sunday 14th December.

[*December 15th,*] *Monday*. Baking and starching.

[*December 16th,*] *Tuesday*. Ironing — the Lloyds called.

[*December 17th,*] *Wednesday*. A very fine day. Writing all the morning for William.

[*December 18th,*] *Thursday*. Mrs. Coleridge and Derwent came. Sweeping chimneys.

[*December 19th,*] *Friday*. Baking.

[*December 20th,*] *Saturday*. Coleridge came. Very ill, rheumatic, feverish. Rain incessantly.

[*December 22nd,*] *Monday*. S. and Wm. went to Lloyd's. Wm. dined. It rained very hard when he came home at . . .

[*This last sentence is probably continued in a volume which has since been lost and which presumably contains entries for the period December 23rd, 1800 to October 9th, 1801.*]

Rydal Falls, by Joseph Wright

II. *October 10th, 1801, to January 16th, 1803*

October 10th, Saturday. Coleridge went to Keswick, after we had built Sara's seat.

[*October*] 11*th, Sunday*. Mr and Miss Simpson came in after tea and supped with us.

[*October*] 12*th, Monday*. We drank tea at Mr. Simpson's.

[*October*] 13*th, Tuesday*. A thorough wet day.

[*October*] 15*th, Thursday*. Dined at Mr. Luff's. A rainy morning. Coleridge came into Mr. Luff's while we were at dinner. Wm. and I walked up Loughrigg Fell, then by the waterside. I held my head under a spout — very sick and ill when I got home, went to bed in the sitting room — took laudanum.

[*October*] 16*th, Friday*. Tom Hutchinson came. It rained almost all day. Coleridge poorly.

[*October*] 17*th, Saturday*. We walked into Easedale. Coleridge poorly after dinner.

[*October*] 18*th, Sunday*. I have forgotten.

[*October*] 19*th, Monday*. Coleridge went home. Tom and William walked to Rydale — a very fine day. I was ill in bed all day. Mr. Simpson tea and supper.

[*October*] 20*th, Tuesday*. We went to the Langdales and Colleth — a very fine day; a heavy shower in the afternoon in Langdale.

[*October*] 21*st, Wednesday*. Dined at Bowness, slept at Penny Bridge — in danger of being cast away on Windermere. A very fine day, but windy a little — a moonlight night.

[*October*] 22*nd, Thursday*. Breakfasted at Penny Bridge — dined at Coniston. A grand stormy day. Drank tea at home.

[*October*] 23*rd, Friday*. A sweet delightful morning. I planted all sorts of plants, Tom helped me. He and W. then rode to Hawkeshead. I baked bread and pies. Tom brought me 2 shrubs from Mr. Curwen's nursery.

[*October*] 24*th, Saturday*. Attempted Fairfield, but misty, and we went no further than Green Head Gill to the sheepfold; mild, misty, beautiful, soft. Wm. and Tom put out the boat — brought the coat from Mr. Luff's. Mr. Simpson came in at dinner-time — drank tea with us and played at cards.

[*October*] 25*th, Sunday*. Rode to Legberthwaite with Tom, expecting Mary — sweet day. Went upon Helvellyn, glorious glorious sights. The sea at Cartmel. The Scotch mountains beyond the sea to the right. Whiteside large, and round, and very soft, and green, behind us. Mists above and below, and close to us, with the Sun amongst them. They shot down to the coves. Left John Stanley's at 10 minutes past 12. Returned thither at ¼ past 4, drank tea, ate heartily. Before we went on Helvellyn we got bread and cheese — Paid 4/- for the whole. Reached home at nine o'clock. A soft grey evening; the light of the moon, but she did not shine on us.

The Windermere Ferry, by John 'Warwick' Smith

October 26th, Monday. Omitted. They went to Buttermere.

October 27th, Tuesday. Omitted, drank tea at the Simpsons.

[October] 28th, Wednesday. The Clarksons came.

[October] 29th, Thursday. Rain all day.

[October] 30th, Friday. Rain all day.

[October] 31st, Saturday. We walked to Rydale — a soft and mild morning, but threatening for rain.

November 1st, Sunday. Very cold — we walked in the evening to Butterlip How.

[November] 2nd, Monday. Very rainy.

[November] 3rd, Tuesday. We dined at Lloyd's. Cold and clear day.

[November] 4th, Wednesday. Mr. C. and Wm. rode out — very cold.

[November 9th, Monday]. . . . The mountains for ever varying, now hid in the clouds, and now with their tops visible while perhaps they were half concealed below — Legberthwaite beautiful. We ate bread and cheese at John Stanley's, and reached Keswick without fatigue just before dark. We enjoyed ourselves in the study and were *at home*. Supped at Mr. Jackson's. Mary and I sate in C.'s room a while.

[November] 10th, Tuesday. Poor C. left us, and we came home together. We left Keswick at 2 o'clock and did not arrive at G. till 9 o'clock. Drank tea at John Stanley's very comfortably. I burnt myself with Coleridge's aquafortis. Mary's

Windermere from Troutbeck,
by J. C. Ibbetson

feet sore. C. had a sweet day for his ride. Every sight and every sound reminded me of him — dear, dear fellow, of his many walks to us by day and by night, of all dear things. I was melancholy, and could not talk, but at last I eased my heart by weeping — nervous blubbering, says William. It is not so. O! how many, many reasons have I to be anxious for him.

[*November*] 11*th, Wednesday*. Baked bread and giblet pie — put books in order — mended stockings. Put aside dearest C.'s letters, and now at about 7 o'clock we are all sitting by a nice fire. Wm. with his book and a candle, and Mary writing to Sara.

November 12th, Thursday. A beautiful still sunshiny morning. We rose very late. I put the rag-boxes into order. We walked out while the goose was roasting — we walked to the top of the hill. M. and I followed Wm. — he was walking upon the turf between John's Grove and the lane. It was a most sweet noon. We did not go into John's Grove but we walked among the rocks and there we sate. Mr. Oliff passed Mary and me upon the road — Wm. still among the rocks. The lake beautiful from the orchard. Wm. and I walked out before tea — The crescent moon — we sate in the slate quarry — I sate there a long time alone. Wm. reached home before me — I found them at tea. There were a thousand stars in the sky.

[*November 13th,*] *Friday Morning.* Dullish, damp and cloudy — a day that promises not to dry our clothes. We spent a happy evening — went to bed late, and had a restless night — Wm. better than I expected.

[*November 14th,*] *Saturday Morning.* Still a cloudy dull day, very dark. I lay in bed all the day very unwell: they made me some broth and I rose better, after it was dark we spent a quiet evening by the fire.

[*November*] *15th, Sunday.* I walked in the morning, to Churnmilk Force nearly, and went upon Heifer Crags. The valley of its winter yellow, but the bed of the brook still in some places almost *shaded* with leaves — the oaks brown in general, but one that might be almost called green — the whole prospect was very soft, and the distant view down the vale very impressive, a long vale down to Ambleside, the hills at Ambleside in mist and sunshine — all else grey. We sate by the fire and read Chaucer (Thomson, Mary read) and Bishop Hall. Letters from Sara and Mrs. Clarkson late at night.

November 16th, Monday. A very darkish misty wettish morning. Mary and Molly ironed all day. I made bread and called at Mr. Olliff's — Mrs O. at home — the prospect soft from the windows. Mrs. O. observed that it was beautiful *even* in winter! The Luffs passed us. We walked backwards and forwards in the Church field. Wm. somewhat weakish, but upon the whole pretty well; he is now, at 7 o'clock, reading Spenser. Mary is writing beside me. The little syke[1] murmurs. We are quiet and happy, but poor Peggy Ashburner is very ill and in pain. She coughs, as if she would cough her life away. I am going to write to Coleridge and Sara. Poor C.! I hope

1. A Lake-country word for a small stream.

he was in London yesterday. Molly has been very witty with Mary all day. She says: "ye may say what ye will, but there's naething like a gay auld man for behaving weel to a young wife. Ye may laugh, but this wind blows no [?] and where there's no love there's no favour." On Sunday I lectured little John Dawson for telling lies — I told him I had heard that he charged Jenny Baty falsely with having beaten him. Says Molly: "she says it's not so, that she never lifted hand till him, and she *should* speak truth you would think in her condition" — she is with child. Two Beggars to-day.

[*November*] *17th, Tuesday.* A very rainy morning. We walked into Easedale before dinner. Miss S. came in at dinner time — we went to Mr. Gell's cottage — then returned. The coppices a beautiful brown. The oaks many, a very fine leafy shade. We stood a long time to look at the corner birch tree. The wind was among the light thin twigs, and they yielded to it, this way and that. Drank tea and supped at the Simpsons — a moonlight wettish night. Dirty roads.

[*November*] *18th, Wednesday.* We sate in the house in the morning reading Spenser. I was unwell and lay in bed all the afternoon. Wm. and Mary walked to Rydale. Very pleasant moonlight. The Lakes beautiful. The church an image of peace. Wm. wrote some lines upon it in bed when they came home. Mary and I walked as far as Sara's Gate before supper. We stood there a long time, the whole scene impressive, the mountains indistinct, the Lake calm and partly ruffled.

Large Island, a sweet sound of water falling into the quiet Lake. A storm was gathering in Easedale, so we returned; but the moon came out, and opened to us the church and village. Helm Crag in shade, the larger mountains dappled like a sky. We stood long upon the bridge. Wished for Wm., he had stayed at home being sickish — found him better; we went to bed.

Nov[embe]r 19th, Thursday.—A beautiful sunny, frosty morning. We did not walk all day. Wm. said he would put it off till the fine moonlight night, and then it came on a heavy rain and wind. Charles and Olivia Lloyd called in the morning.

[November] 20th, Friday. We walked in the morning to Easedale. In the evening we had chearful letters from Coleridge and Sara.

[November] 21st, Saturday. We walked in the morning, and paid one pound and 4d. for letters. William out of spirits. We had a pleasant walk and spent a pleasant evening. There was a furious wind and cold at night. Mr. Simpson drank tea with us, and helped William out with the boat. Wm. and Mary walked to the Swan, homewards, with him. A keen clear frosty night. I went into the orchard while they were out.

[November] 22nd, Sunday.—We wrote to Coleridge and sent our letter by the boy. Mr. and Miss Simpson came in at tea time. We went with them to the Blacksmith's and returned by Butterlip How — a frost and wind with bright

Grasmere Church, and Churchyard.

Interior of Smithy, Ambleside, by John Harden

moonshine. The vale looked spacious and very beautiful — the level meadows seemed very large and some nearer us, unequal ground, heaving like sand, the Cottages beautiful and quiet, we passed one near which stood a cropped ash with upright forked branches like the Devil's horns frightening a guilty conscience. We were happy and chearful when we came home — we went early to bed.

Nov[ember] 23rd, Monday. A beautiful frosty morning. Mary was making William's woollen waistcoat. Wm. unwell, and did not walk. Mary and I sate in our cloaks upon the bench in the orchard. After dinner I went to bed unwell. Mary had a headach at night. We all went to bed soon.

[November] 24th, Tuesday. A rainy morning. We all were well except that my head ached a little, and I took my breakfast in bed. I read a little of Chaucer, prepared the goose for dinner, and then we all walked out. I was obliged to return for my fur tippet and spencer, it was so cold. We had intended going to Easedale, but we shaped our course to Mr. Gell's cottage. It was very windy, and we heard the wind everywhere about us as we went along the lane, but the walls sheltered us. John Green's house looked pretty under Silver How. As we were going along we stopped at once, at the distance perhaps of 50 yards from our favourite birch tree. It was yielding to the gusty wind with all its tender twigs, the sun shone upon it, and it glanced in the wind like a flying sunshiny shower. It was a tree in

shape, with stem and branches, but it was like a Spirit of water. The sun went in, and it resumed its purplish appearance, the twigs still yielding to the wind, but not so visibly to us. The other birch trees that were near it looked bright and chearful, but it was a creature by its own self among them. We could not get into Mr. Gell's grounds—the old tree fallen from its undue exaltation above the gate. A shower came on when we were at Benson's. We went through the wood—it became fair. There was a rainbow which spanned the lake from the island-house to the foot of Bainriggs. The village looked populous and beautiful. Catkins are coming out; palm trees budding; the alder, with its plumb-coloured buds. We came home over the stepping-stones. The lake was foamy with white waves. I saw a solitary butter-flower in the wood. I found it not easy to get over the stepping stones.[1] Reached home at dinner time. Sent Peggy Ashburner some goose. She sent me some honey, with a thousand thanks. "Alas! the gratitude of men has", etc. I

1. At the head of Rydal Water, now superseded by Slater's Bridge.

went in to set her right about this, and sate a while with her. She talked about Thomas's having sold his land. "Ay," says she, "I said many a time he's not come fra London to buy our land, however." Then she told me with what pains and industry they had made up their taxes, interest, etc. etc., how they all got up at 5 o'clock in the morning to spin and Thomas carded, and that they had paid off a hundred pounds of the interest. She said she used to take such pleasure in the cattle and sheep. "O how pleased I used to be when they fetched them down, and when I had been a bit poorly I would gang out upon a hill and look ower 't fields and see them, and it used to do me so much good you cannot think." Molly said to me when I came in, "Poor body! she's very ill, but one does not know how long she may last. Many a fair face may gang before her." We sate by the fire without work for some time, then Mary read a poem of Daniel upon Learning. After tea Wm. read Spenser, now and then a little aloud to us. We were making his waistcoat. We had a note from Mrs. C., with bad news from poor C.—very ill. William went to John's Grove. I went to meet him. Moonlight, but it rained. I met him before I had got as far as John Baty's — he had been surprized and terrified by a sudden rushing of winds, which seemed to bring earth sky and lake together, as if the whole were going to enclose him in; he was glad he was in a high road.

In speaking of our walk on Sunday evening, the 22nd November, I forgot to notice one most impressive sight. It was the moon and the moonlight seen through hurrying driving clouds immediately behind the Stone-Man upon the top of the hill on the Forest Side. Every tooth and every edge of rock was visible, and the Man stood like a Giant watching from the roof of a lofty castle. The hill seemed perpendicular from the darkness below it. It was a sight that I could call to mind at any time, it was so distinct.

November 25th, Wednesday. It was a showery morning and threatened to be a wettish day, but the sun shone once or twice. We were engaged to the Lloyds and Wm. and Mary were determined to go that it might be over. I accompanied them to the thorn beside Rydale water. I parted from them first at the top of the hill,

Woman Spinning, by John Harden

and they called me back. It rained a little, and rained afterwards all the afternoon. I baked pies and bread, and wrote to Sara Hutchinson and Coleridge. I passed a pleasant evening, but the wind roared so, and it was such a storm that I was afraid for them. They came in at nine o'clock, no worse for their walk, and chearful, blooming, and happy.

[*November*] *26th, Thursday.* Mr. Olliff called before Wm. was up to say that they would drink tea with us this afternoon. We walked into Easedale, to gather mosses, and to fetch cream. I went for the cream, and they sate under a wall. It was piercing cold and a hailstorm came on in the afternoon. The Olliffs arrived at 5 o'clock. We played at cards and passed a decent evening. It was a very still night but piercing cold when they went away at 11 o'clock — a shower came on.

November 27th, Friday. Snow upon the ground thinly scattered. It snowed after we got up, and then the sun shone, and it was very warm though frosty—now the sun shines sweetly. A woman came who was travelling with her husband; he had been wounded and was going with her to live at Whitehaven. She had been at Ambleside the night before, offered 4d at the Cock for a bed — they sent her to one Harrison's where she and her husband had slept upon the hearth and bought a pennyworth of chips for a fire. Her husband was gone before, very lame — "Aye" says she, "I was once an officer's wife, I, as you see me now. My first husband married me at Appleby; I had 18£ a year for teaching a school, and

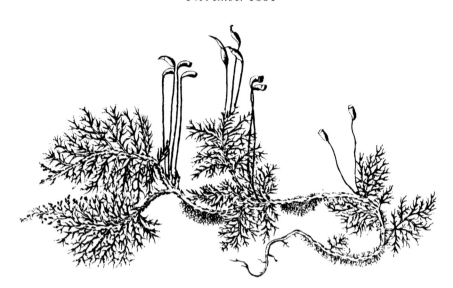

because I had no fortune his father turned him out of doors. I have been in the West Indies. I lost the use of this finger just before he died; he came to me and said he must bid farewell to his dear children and me. I had a muslin gown on like yours — I seized hold of his coat as he went from me, and slipped the joint of my finger. He was shot directly. I came to London and married this man. He was clerk to Judge Chambray, *that man,* that man that's going on the road now. If he, Judge Chambray, had been at Kendal he would [have] given us a guinea or two, and made nought of it, for he is very generous." Before dinner we set forward to walk intending to return to dinner, but as we had got as far as Rydale Wm. thought he would go on to Mr. Luff's. We accompanied him under Loughrigg, and parted near the stepping stones. It was very cold. Mary and I walked quick home. There was a fine gleam of sunshine upon the eastern side of Ambleside Vale. We came up the old road and turning round we were struck with the appearance. Mary wrote to her aunt. We expected the Simpsons. I was sleepy and weary and went to bed before tea. It came on wet in the evening and was very cold. We expected letters from C. and Sara — Sara's came by the boy, but none from C. — a sad disappointment. We did not go to meet Wm. as we had intended — Mary was at work at Wm.'s warm waistcoat.

November 28th, Saturday.—A very fine sunny morning. Soldiers still going by. I should have mentioned that yesterday when we went with Wm. to Mr. Luff's we met a soldier and his wife, he with a child in his arms, she carrying a bundle and his gun — we gave them some halfpence, it was such a pretty sight. William having slept ill lay in bed till after one o'clock. Mary and I walked up to Mr. Simpson's between 20 minutes before 2 and 20 minutes before 3 to desire them not to come. We drank tea and supped at Mr. Olliff's — a keen frost and sparkling stars when we came home at ½ past 11.

November 29th, Sunday. Baking bread, apple pies and giblet pie — a bad giblet pie. It was a most beautiful morning. George Olliff brought Wm.'s stick. The sun shone all the day, but we never walked. In the evening we had intended going for letters, but the lad said he would go. We sate up till after one — no letters! very cold — hard frost.

[*November*] 30*th, Monday.* A fine sharp morning. The lad brought us a letter from Montagu, and a short one from Coleridge. C. very well, promised to write to-morrow. We walked round the Lake, Wm. and Mary went first over the stepping stones — I remained after them and went into the prospect field above Benson's to sit — Mary joined me there. Clear and frosty without wind. William went before to look at Langdale. We saw the Pikes and then came home. They have cropped the tree which overshadowed the gate beside that cottage at the turning of the hill which used to make a frame for Loughrigg Tarn and Winder-mere. We came home and read — Mary wrote to Joanna — I wrote to Richard, and Mrs. Coleridge.

December 1st, 1801, Tuesday. A fine sunny and frosty morning. Mary and I walked to Rydale for letters. William was not well and staid at home reading after having lain long in bed. We found a letter from Coleridge, a short one — he was pretty well. We were overtaken by two soldiers on our return — one of them being very drunk we wished them to pass us, but they had too much liquor in them to go very fast so we contrived to pass them — they were very merry and very civil. They fought with the mountains with their sticks. "Aye" says one, "that will [? fall] upon us. One might stride over that etc." They never saw such a wild country, though one of them was a Scotchman. They were honest looking fellows. The Corporal said he was frightened to see the road before them. We met Wm. at Sara's gate — he went back intending to go round the lake, but having attempted to cross the water and not succeeding he came back. The Simpsons, Mr. and Miss, drank tea with us — Wm. was very poorly and out of spirits. They stayed supper.

[*December*] 2*nd, Wednesday.* A fine grey frosty morning. Wm. rose late. I read the Tale of Phœbus and the Crow, which he afterwards attempted to translate, and did translate a large part of it to-day. Mrs. Olliff brought us some yeast and made us promise to go there the next day to meet the Luffs. We were sitting by the fire in the evening when Charles and Olivia Lloyd came in. I had not been very well so I did not venture out with them when they went away — Mary and William went as far as Rydale village. It snowed after it was dark and there was a thin covering over the ground which made it light and soft. They looked fresh and well when they came in. I wrote part of a letter to Coleridge. After his return William went on a little with Chaucer.

December 3rd, 1801, Thursday. I was not well in the morning — we baked bread — after dinner I went to bed — Wm. walked into Easedale. Rain, hail and snow. I rose at ½ past 7, got tea, then went to sup at Mr. Olliff's — I had a glorious sleep and was quite well. A light night, roads very slippery. We spent a pleasant evening — Mr. and Mrs. Luff there — Mrs. L. poorly. I wrote a little bit of my letter to Coleridge before I went to Mr. O.'s. We went to bed immediately after our return — Molly gone.

Slate Quarry,

by W. H. Pyne

[*December*] *4th, Friday.* My head bad and I lay long. Mrs. Luff called — Mary went with her to the slate quarry. Mr. Simpson and Charles Lloyd called for the yeast receipt. William translating *The Prioress's Tale.* William and Mary walked after tea to Rydale. It snowed and rained and they came in wet. I finished the letter to Coleridge, and we received a letter from him and Sara. S.'s letter written in good spirits — C.'s also. A letter of Lamb's about George Dyer with it.

[*December*] *5th, Saturday.* My head bad and I lay long. Mr. Luff called before I rose. We put off walking in the morning, dull and misty and grey — very rainy in the afternoon and we could not go out. Wm. finished *The Prioress's Tale,* and after tea Mary and he wrote it out. Wm. not well. No parcel from Mrs. Coleridge.

[*December*] *6th, Sunday.* A very fine beautiful sunshiny morning. Wm. worked a while at Chaucer, then we set forward to walk into Easedale. We met Mr. and Mrs. Olliff who were going to call upon us; they turned back with us and we parted at the White Bridge. We went up into Easedale and walked backwards and forwards in that flat field, which makes the second circle of Easedale, with that beautiful rock in the field beside us, and all the rocks and the woods and the mountains enclosing us round. The sun was shining among them, the snow thinly scattered upon the tops of the mountains. In the afternoon we sate by the fire: I read Chaucer aloud, and Mary read the first canto of *The Fairy Queen.* After tea Mary and I walked to Ambleside for letters — reached home by 11 o'clock — we had a sweet walk. It was a sober starlight evening, the stars not shining as it were with all their brightness when they were visible, and sometimes hiding themselves behind small greyish clouds, that passed soberly along. We opened C.'s letter at Wilcock's door. We thought we saw that he wrote in good spirits, so

Slate-wharf, Clappersgate, by R. R. Reinagle

we came happily homewards where we arrived 2 hours after we left home. It was a sad melancholy letter, and prevented us all from sleeping.

December 7th, Monday Morning. We rose by candlelight. A showery unpleasant morning, after a downright rainy night. We determined, however, to go to Keswick if possible, and we set off at a little after 9 o'clock. When we were upon the Rays, it snowed very much; and the whole prospect closed in upon us, like a moorland valley, upon a moor very wild. But when we were at the top of the Rays we saw the mountains before us. The sun shone upon them, here and there; and Wytheburn vale, though wild, looked soft. The [? day] went on chearfully and pleasantly. Now and then a hail shower attacked us; but we kept up a good heart, for Mary is a famous jockey. We met Miss Barcroft — she had been unwell in the "*Liverpool* complaint", and was riding out for the benefit of her health. She had not seen Mrs. C. "The weather had been such as to preclude all intercourse between neighbours!" We reached Greta Hall at about one o'clock, met Mrs. C. in the field, Derwent in the cradle asleep — Hartley at his dinner — Derwent pale, the image of his Father. Hartley well. We wrote to C. Mrs. C. left us at ½ past 2. We drank tea by ourselves, the children playing about us. Mary said to Hartley, "Shall I take Derwent with me?" "No," says H., "I cannot spare my little Brother," in the sweetest tone possible, "and he can't do without his mamma." "Well," says Mary, "why can't I be his mamma? Can't he have more mammas than one?" "No," says H. "What for?" "Because they do not love, and mothers do." "What is the difference between mothers and mammas?" Looking at his sleeves, "Mothers wear sleeves like this," (pulling his own tight down), "and mammas" (pulling them up, and making a bustle about his shoulders) "so". We parted from them at 4 o'clock. It was a little of the dusk when we set off. Cotton mills lighted up. The first star at Nadel Fell, but it was never dark. We rode very briskly. Snow upon the Rays. Reached home far sooner than we expected — at seven o'clock. William at work with Chaucer, *The God of Love*. Sate latish. I wrote a letter to C.

December 8th, 1801, Tuesday. A dullish, rainyish morning. Wm. at work with Chaucer. I read Bruce's *Lochleven* and *Life*. Going to bake bread and pies. After dinner I felt myself unwell having not slept well in the night, so, after we had put up the Bookcases which Charles Lloyd sent us, I lay down — I did not sleep much but I rose refreshed. Mary and William walked to the boat house at Rydale while I was in bed. It rained very hard all night. No company. Wm. worked at *The Cuckow and the Nightingale* till he was tired. Mary very sleepy and not quite well. We both slept sound. Letter from Richard with news of John, dated 7th August.

December 9th, Wednesday Morning. William slept well, but his tongue [? furred]. I read *Palamon and Arcite*. Mary read Bruce. William writing out his alteration of Chaucer's *Cuckow and Nightingale*. After dinner it was agreed that we should walk — when I had finished a letter to C. part of which I had written in the morning by the kitchen fire while the mutton was roasting. Wm. did not go with us but Mary and I walked into Easedale, and backwards and forwards in that large field under George Rawnson's white cottage. We had intended gathering mosses, and for that purpose we turned into the green lane, behind the tailor's, but it was too dark to see the mosses. The river came galloping past the Church, as fast it could come; and when we got into Easedale we saw Churn Milk Force, like a broad stream of snow. At the little footbridge we stopped to look at the company of rivers, which came hurrying down the vale this way and that; it was a valley of streams and islands, with that great waterfall at the head, and lesser falls in different parts of the mountains, coming down to these rivers. We could hear the sound of those lesser falls, but we could not *see* them. We walked backwards and forwards till all distant objects, except the white shape of the waterfall and the lines of the mountains, were gone. We had the crescent moon when we went out, and at our return there were a few stars that shone dimly, but it was a grey cloudy night.

December 10th, Thursday. A very fine sunny morning — not frosty. We walked into Easedale to gather mosses, and then we went past to Aggy Fleming's and up the Gill, beyond that little waterfall. It was a wild scene of crag and mountain. One craggy point rose above the rest irregular and rugged, and very impressive it was. We called at Aggy Fleming's — she told us about her miserable house — she looked shockingly with her head tied up. Her mother was there — the children looked healthy. We were very unsuccessful in our search after mosses. Just when the evening was closing in, Mr. Clarkson came to the door. It was a fine frosty evening. We played at cards.

Entrance to Easedale, by Thomas Austin

[*December*] 11*th, Friday.* Baked pies and cakes. It was a stormy morning with hail showers. The Luffs dined with us — Mrs. L. came with Mrs. Olliff in the gig. We sate lazily round the fire after dinner. Mr. and Mrs. Olliff drank tea and supped with us — a hard frost when they came.

[*December*] 12*th, Saturday.* A fine frosty morning — Snow upon the ground. I made bread and pies. We walked with Mrs. Luff to Rydale and came home the other side of the Lake, met Townley with his dogs. All looked chearful and bright. Helm Crag rose very bold and craggy, a Being by itself, and behind it was the large ridge of mountain, smooth as marble and snow white. All the mountains looked like solid stone, on our left, going from Grasmere, *i.e.* White Moss and Nab Scar. The snow hid all the grass, and all signs of vegetation, and the rocks showed themselves boldly everywhere, and seemed more stony than rock or stone. The birches on the crags beautiful, red brown and glittering. The ashes glittering spears with their upright stems. The hips very beautiful, and so good!! and, dear Coleridge! I ate twenty for thee, when I was by myself. I came home first — they walked too slow for me. Wm. went to look at Langdale Pikes. We had a sweet invigorating walk. Mr. Clarkson came in before tea. We played at cards — sate up late. The moon shone upon the water below Silver-How, and above it hung, combining with Silver-How on one side, a bowl-shaped moon, the curve downwards; the white fields, glittering roof of Thomas Ashburner's

The Quill Winder, by John Harden

house, the dark yew tree, the white fields gay and beautiful. Wm. lay with his curtains open that he might see it.

[*December*] 13*th, Sunday.* Mr. Clarkson left us, leading his horse. Went to Brathay and Luffs. We drank tea at Betty Dixon's. Very cold and frosty — a pleasant walk home. Wm. had been very unwell, but we found him better. The boy brought letters from Coleridge, and from Sara. Sara in bad spirits about C.

December 14*th, Monday.* Wm. and Mary walked to Ambleside in the morning to buy mouse-traps. Mary fell and hurt her wrist. I accompanied them to the top of the hill — clear and frosty. I wrote to Coleridge a very long letter while they were absent. Sate by the fire in the evening reading.

[*December*] 15*th,* Tuesday. Wm. and I walked to Rydale for letters — found one from Joanna. We had a pleasant walk but coldish — it thawed a little.

[*December*] 16*th, Wednesday.* A very keen frost, extremely slippery. After dinner Wm. and I walked twice up to the Swan and back again — met Miss Simpson. She came with us to Olliff's and we went back with her. Very cold.

[*December*] 17*th, Thursday.* Snow in the night and still snowing. We went to Mr. Luff's to dine — met Mrs. King. Hard frost and as light as day — we had a delightful walk and reached home a little after twelve. Mrs. Luff ill. Ambleside looked excessively beautiful as we came out — like a village in another country; and the light chearful mountains were seen in the long, long distance as bright and as clear as at midday with the blue sky above them. We heard waterfowl calling out by the lake side. Jupiter was very glorious above the Ambleside hills, and one large star hung over the coombe of the hills on the opposite side of Rydale water.

December 18th, 1801, Friday. Mary and Wm. walked round the two lakes. I staid at home to make bread, cakes and pies. I afterwards went to meet them, and I met Wm. near Benson's. Mary had gone to look at Langdale Pikes. It was a chearful glorious day. The birches and all trees beautiful, hips bright red, mosses green. I wrote to Coleridge for money.

[*December*] *19th, Saturday.* I was not quite well and did not rise to breakfast. We walked by Brathay to Ambleside — called at the Lloyds — they were at Kendal. Dined with the Luffs and came home in the evening — the evening cloudy and promising snow. The day very beautiful — Brathay vale scattered and very chearful and interesting.

December 20th, Sunday. It snowed all day. In the evening we went to tea at Thomas Ashburner's. It was a very deep snow. The brooms were very beautiful, arched feathers with wiry stalks pointed to the end, smaller and smaller. They waved gently with the weight of the snow. We stayed at Thomas A.'s till after 9 o'clock — Peggy better. The lasses neat and clean and rosy.

Monday 21st, being the shortest day. Mary walked to Ambleside for letters. It was a wearisome walk, for the snow lay deep upon the roads and it was beginning to thaw. I stayed at home and clapped the small linen. Wm. sate beside me, and read *The Pedlar.* He was in good spirits, and full of hope of what he should do with it. He went to meet Mary, and they brought 4 letters — 2 from Coleridge, one from Sara, and one from France. Coleridge's were melancholy letters, he had been very ill in his bowels. We were made very unhappy. Wm. wrote to him, and

Group Writing and Reading, by John Harden

directed the letter into Somersetshire. I finished it after tea. In the afternoon Mary and I ironed, afterwards she packed her clothes up, and I mended Wm.'s stockings while he was reading *The Pedlar*. I then packed up for Mr. Clarkson's — we carried the boxes cross the road to Fletcher's [? peat] house, after Mary had written to Sara and Joanna.

[*December*] 22*nd, Tuesday*. Still thaw. I washed my head. Wm. and I went to Rydale for letters, the road was covered with dirty snow, rough and rather slippery. We had a melancholy letter from C., for he had been very ill, though he was better when he wrote. We walked home almost without speaking. Wm. composed a few lines of *The Pedlar*. We talked about Lamb's tragedy as we went down the White Moss. We stopped a long time in going to watch a little bird with a salmon-coloured breast, a white cross or T upon its wings, and a brownish back with faint stripes. It was pecking the scattered dung upon the road. It began to peck at the distance of four yards from us, and advanced nearer and nearer till it came within the length of Wm.'s stick, without any apparent fear of us. As we came up the White Moss, we met an old man, who I saw was a beggar by his two bags hanging over his shoulder; but, from a half laziness, half indifference, and a wanting to *try* him, if he would speak, I let him pass. He said nothing, and my heart smote me. I turned back, and said, "You are begging?" "Ay", says he. I gave him a halfpenny. William, judging from his appearance, joined in, "I suppose you were a sailor?" "Ay", he replied, "I have been 57 years at sea, 12 of them on board a man-of-war under Sir Hugh Palmer." "Why have you not a pension?" "I have no pension, but I could have got into Greenwich hospital, but all my officers are dead." He was 75 years of age, had a freshish colour in his cheeks, grey hair, a decent hat with a binding round the edge, the hat worn brown and glossy, his shoes were small thin shoes low in the quarters, pretty

CHAFFINCH.

good. They had belonged to a gentleman. His coat was blue, frock shaped, coming over his thighs, it had been joined up at the seams behind with paler blue, to let it out, and there were three bell-shaped patches of darker blue behind, where the buttons had been. His breeches were either of fustian, or grey cloth, with strings hanging down, whole and tight; he had a checked shirt on, and a small còloured handkerchief tied round his neck. His bags were hung over each shoulder, and lay on each side of him, below his breast. One was brownish and of coarse stuff, the other was white with meal on the outside, and his blue waistcoat was whitened with meal. In the coarse bag I guess he put his scraps of meat etc. He walked with a slender stick — decently stout, but his legs bowed outwards.

We overtook old Fleming at Rydale, leading his little Dutchman-like grand-child along the slippery road. The same pace seemed to be natural to them both, the old man and the little child, and they went hand in hand, the grandfather cautious, yet looking proud of his charge. He had two patches of new cloth at the shoulder-blades of his faded claret-coloured coat, like eyes at each shoulder not worn elsewhere. I found Mary at home in her riding-habit, all her clothes being put up. We were very sad about Coleridge. Wm. walked further. When he came home he cleared a path to the necessary, called me out to see it, but before we got there a whole housetopfull of snow had fallen from the roof upon the path and it echoed in the ground beneath like a dull beating upon it. We talked of going to

Ambleside after dinner to borrow money of Luff, but we thought we would defer our visit to Eusemere a day. Half the seaman's nose was reddish as if he had been in his youth somewhat used to drinking, though he was not injured by it. We stopped to look at the stone seat at the top of the hill. There was a white cushion upon it, round at the edge like a cushion, and the rock behind looked soft as velvet, of a vivid green, and so tempting! The snow too looked as soft as a down cushion. A young foxglove, like a star, in the centre. There were a few green lichens about it, and a few withered brackens of fern here and there upon the ground near, all else was a thick snow; no footmark to it, not the foot of a sheep. When we were at Thomas Ashburner's on Sunday Peggy talked about the Queen of Patterdale. She had been brought to drinking by her husband's unkindness and avarice. She was formerly a very nice tidy woman. She had taken to drinking but that was better than if she had taken to something worse (by this I suppose she meant killing herself). She said that her husband used to be out all night with other women and she used to *hear* him coming in in the morning, for they never slept together — "Many a poor body, a wife like me, has had a working heart for her, as much stuff as she had". We sate snugly round the fire. I read to them the Tale of Custance and the Syrian monarch, also some of the *Prologues*. It is the Man of Lawe's Tale. We went to bed early. It snowed and thawed.

[*December*] *23rd, Wednesday*. A downright thaw, but the snow not gone off the ground except on the steep hillsides — it was a thick black heavy air. I baked pies and bread. Mary wrote out the Tales from Chaucer for Coleridge. William worked at *The Ruined Cottage* and made himself very ill. I went to bed without dinner — he went to the other bed — we both slept and Mary lay on the rug before the fire. A broken soldier came to beg in the morning. Afterwards a tall woman, dressed somewhat in a tawdry style, with a long checked muslin apron, a beaver hat, and throughout what are called good clothes. Her daughter had gone before, with a soldier and his wife. She had buried her husband at Whitehaven, and was going back into Cheshire.

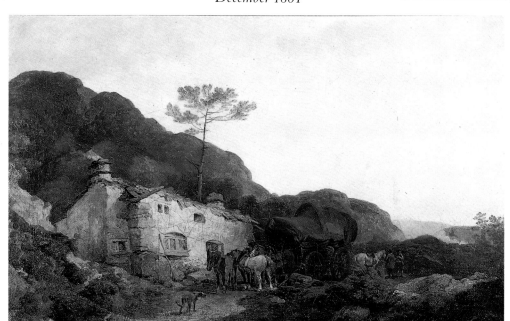

Cottage at Patterdale, by P. J. de Loutherbourg

[*December*] 24th, *Thursday*. Still a thaw. We walked to Rydale, Wm. Mary and I — left the patterns at Thomas Fleming's for Mrs. King. The roads uncomfortable and slippery. We sate comfortably round the fire in the evening, and read Chaucer. Thoughts of last year. I took out my old Journal.

[*December*] 25th, *Friday*. Christmas Day. A very bad day — we drank tea at John Fisher's — we were unable to walk. I went to bed after dinner. The roads very slippery. We received a letter from Coleridge while we were at John Fisher's — a terrible night — little John brought the letter. Coleridge poorly but better — his letter made us uneasy about him. I was glad I was not by myself when I received it.

[*December*] 26th, *Saturday*. My head ached and I lay long in bed and took my breakfast there — soon after I had breakfasted we went to call at Mr. Olliff's. They were not at home. It came on very wet. Mary went into the house, and Wm. and I went up to Tom Dawson's to speak about his Grandchild, the rain went off and we walked to Rydale. It was very pleasant — Grasmere Lake a beautiful image of stillness, clear as glass, reflecting all things, the wind was up, and the waters sounding. The lake of a rich purple, the fields a soft yellow, the island yellowish-green, the copses red-brown, the mountains purple. The Church and buildings, how quiet they were! Poor Coleridge, Sara, and dear little Derwent here last year at this time. After tea we sate by the fire comfortably. I read

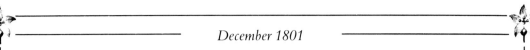

aloud *The Miller's Tale*. Wrote to Coleridge. The Olliffs passed in chaise and gig. Wm. wrote part of the poem to Coleridge.

[*December*] *27th, Sunday*. A fine soft beautiful, mild day, with gleams of sunshine. I lay in bed till 12 o'clock, Mr. Clarkson's man came — we wrote to him. We walked up within view of Rydale. William went to take in his Boat. I sate in John's Grove a little while. Mary came home. Mary wrote some lines of the third part of Wm.'s poem, which he brought to read to us, when we came home. Mr. Simpson came in at dinner time and stayed tea. They fetched in the boat. I lay down upon the bed in the meantime. A sweet evening.

December 28th, Monday. William, Mary, and I set off on foot to Keswick. We carried some cold mutton in our pockets, and dined at John Stanley's, where they were making Christmas pies. The sun shone, but it was coldish. We parted from Wm. upon the Rays. He joined us opposite Sara's rock. He was busy in composition, and sate down upon the wall. We did not see him again till we arrived at John Stanley's. There we roasted apples in the oven. After we had left John Stanley's, Wm. discovered that he had lost his gloves. He turned back, but they were gone. We were tired and had bad headaches. We rested often. Once he left his Spenser, and Mary turned back for it, and found it upon the bank, where we had last rested. We reached Greta Hall at about ½ past 5 o'clock. The Children and Mrs. C. well. After tea, message came from Wilkinson, who had passed us on the road, inviting Wm. to sup at the Oak. He went. Met a young man (a predestined Marquis) called Johnston. He spoke to him familiarly of the L. B. He had seen a copy presented by the Queen to Mrs. Harcourt. Said he saw them everywhere, and wondered they did not sell. We all went weary to bed — my bowels very bad.

December 29th, Tuesday. A fine morning. A thin fog upon the hills which soon disappeared. The sun shone. Wilkinson went with us to the top of the hill. We turned out of the road at the second mile stone, and passed a pretty cluster of houses at the foot of St. John's Vale. The houses were among tall trees, partly of Scotch fir, and some naked forest trees. We crossed a bridge just below these houses, and the river winded sweetly along the meadows. Our road soon led us along the sides of dreary bare hills, but we had a glorious prospect to the left of Saddleback, half-way covered with snow, and underneath the comfortable white houses and the village of Threlkeld. These houses and the village want trees about them. Skiddaw was behind us, and dear Coleridge's desert home. As we ascended the hills it grew very cold and slippery. Luckily, the wind was at our backs, and helped us on. A sharp hail-shower gathered at the head of Martindale, and the view upwards was very grand — the wild cottages, seen through the hurrying hail-shower. The wind drove and eddied about and about, and the hills looked large and swelling through the storm. We thought of Coleridge. O! the bonny nooks and windings and curlings of the beck, down at the bottom of the steep green mossy banks. We dined at the publick-house on porridge, with a second course of Christmas pies. We were well received by the Landlady, and her little Jewish daughters were glad to see us again. The husband a very handsome man.

Farmer Wilson's, Goody Bridge, Easedale, by Thomas Austin

black, rocks bluish. Before night the Island was quite green; the sun had melted all the snow upon it. Mr. Simpson called before Wm. had done shaving — William had had a bad night and was working at his poem. We sate by the fire, and did not walk, but read *The Pedlar,* thinking it done; but lo! though Wm. could find fault with no one part of it, it was uninteresting, and must be altered. Poor Wm.!

February 8th, 1802, *Monday Morning.* It was very windy and rained very hard all the morning. William worked at his poem and I read a little in Lessing and the grammar. A chaise came past to fetch Ellis the Carrier who had hurt his head.

After dinner (*i.e.* we set off at about ½ past 4) we went towards Rydale for letters. It was a cold *"cauld clash"*. The rain had been so cold that it hardly melted the snow. We stopped at Park's to get some straw in Wm.'s shoes. The young mother was sitting by a bright wood fire with her youngest child upon her lap, and the other two sate on each side of the chimney. The light of the fire made them a beautiful sight, with their innocent countenances, their rosy cheeks, and glossy curling hair. We sate and talked about poor Ellis, and our journey over the Hawes. It had been reported that we came over in the night. Willy told us of 3 men who were once lost in crossing that way in the night; they had carried a lantern with them; the lantern went out at the Tarn, and they all perished. Willy had seen their cloaks drying at the public-house in Patterdale the day before their funeral. We walked on very wet through the clashy cold roads in bad spirits at the idea of having to go as far as Rydale, but before we had come again to the shore of

Keswick and Grisedale Pike, by William Westall

the Lake, we met our patient bow-bent Friend, with his little wooden box at his back. "Where are you going?" said he. "To Rydale for letters." "I have two for you in my box." We lifted up the lid, and there they lay. Poor fellow, he straddled and pushed on with all his might; but we soon outstripped him far away when we had turned back with our letters. We were very thankful that we had not to go on, for we should have been sadly tired. In thinking of this I could not help comparing lots with him! He goes at that slow pace every morning, and after having wrought a hard day's work returns at night, however weary he may be, takes it all quietly, and, though perhaps he neither feels thankfulness nor pleasure, when he eats his supper, and has no luxury to look forward to but falling asleep in bed, yet I daresay he neither murmurs nor thinks it hard. He seems mechanized to labour. We broke the seal of Coleridge's letter, and I had light enough just to see that he was not ill. I put it in my pocket, but at the top of the White Moss I took it to my bosom, a safer place for it. The night was wild. There was a strange mountain lightness, when we were at the top of the White Moss. I have often observed it there in the evenings, being between the two valleys. There is more of the sky than any other place. It has a strange effect sometimes along with the obscurity of evening or night. It seems almost like a peculiar *sort* of light. There was not much wind till we came to John's Grove, then it roared right out of the grove; all the trees were tossing about. C.'s letter somewhat damped us, it spoke with less confidence about France. Wm. wrote to him. The other letter was from

Montagu, with £8. Wm. was very unwell, tired when he had written. He went to bed, and left me to write to M. H., Montagu, and Calvert, and Mrs. Coleridge. I had written in his letter to Coleridge. We wrote to Calvert to beg him not to fetch us on Sunday. Wm. left me with a *little* peat fire — it grew less. I wrote on, and was starved. At 2 o'clock I went to put my letters under Fletcher's door. I never felt such a cold night. There was a strong wind and it froze very hard. I collected together all the clothes I could find (for I durst not go into the pantry for fear of waking William). At first when I went to bed I seemed to be warm. I suppose because the cold air, which I had just left, no longer touched my body; but I soon found that I was mistaken. I could not sleep from sheer cold. I had baked pies and bread in the morning. Coleridge's letter contained prescriptions.

N.B.   The moon came out suddenly when we were at John's Grove, and a star or two besides.

[*February 9th,*] *Tuesday.* Wm. had slept better. He fell to work, and made himself unwell. We did not walk. A funeral came by of a poor woman who had drowned herself, some say because she was hardly treated by her husband; others that he was a very decent respectable man, and *she* but an indifferent wife. However this was, she had only been married to him last Whitsuntide and had had very indifferent health ever since. She had got up in the night, and drowned herself in the pond. She had requested to be buried beside her mother, and so she was brought in a hearse. She was followed by several decent-looking men on horseback, her sister, Thomas Fleming's wife, in a chaise, and some others with her, and a cart full of women. Molly says folks thinks o' their mothers. Poor body, *she* has been little thought of by any body else. We did a little of Lessing. I attempted a fable, but my head ached; my bones were sore with the cold of the day before, and I was downright stupid. We went to bed, but not till Wm. had tired himself.

[*February*] 10th, *Wednesday*. A very snowy morning. It cleared up a little however for a while but we did not walk. We sent for our letters by Fletcher and for some writing paper etc. He brought us word there were none. This was strange for I depended on Mary. While I was writing out the poem, as we hope for a final writing, a letter was brought me by John Dawson's daughter, the letter written at Eusemere. I paid Wm. Jackson's bill by John Fisher, sent off a letter to Montagu by Fletcher. After Molly went we read the first part of the poem and were delighted with it, but Wm. afterwards got to some ugly place, and went to bed tired out. A wild, moonlight night.

[*February*] 11th, *Thursday*. A very fine clear sunny frost, the ground white with snow — William rose before Molly was ready for him, I rose at a little after nine. William sadly tired and working still at *The Pedlar*. Miss Simpson called when he was worn out — he escaped and sate in his own room till she went. She was very faint and ill, had had a tooth drawn and had suffered greatly. I walked up with her past Gawain's. The sun was very warm till we got past Lewthwaite's — then it had little power, and had not melted the roads. As I came back again I felt the vale like a different climate. The vale was bright and beautiful. Molly had linen hung out. We had pork to dinner sent us by Mrs. Simpson. William still poorly. We made up a good fire after dinner, and Wm. brought his mattress out, and lay down on the floor. I read to him the life of Ben Jonson, and some short poems of his, which were too *interesting* for him, and would not let him go to sleep. I had begun with Fletcher, but he was too *dull* for me. Fuller says, in his *Life of Jonson* (speaking of his plays), "If his latter be not so spriteful and vigorous as his first pieces, all that are old, and all who desire to be old, should excuse him therein". He says he *"beheld"* wit-combats between Shakespeare and Jonson, and compares Shakespeare to an English man-of-war, Jonson to a Spanish great galleon. There is one affecting line in Jonson's epitaph on his first daughter —

> *Here lies to each her parents ruth,*
> Mary the daughter of their youth.
> *At six months' end she parted hence,*
> *In safety of her innocence.*

I have been writing this journal while Wm. has had a nice little sleep. Once he was waked by Charles Lloyd who had come to see about lodgings for his children in the hooping cough. It is now 7 o'clock — I have a nice coal fire — Wm. is still on his bed. Two beggars to-day. I continued to read to him. We were much delighted with the poem of *Penshurst*. Wm. rose better. I was chearful and happy. But he got to work again, and went to bed unwell.

[*February*] 12th, *Friday*. A very fine, bright, clear, hard frost. Wm. working again. I recopied *The Pedlar*, but poor Wm. all the time at work. Molly tells me "What! little Sally's gone to visit at Mr. Simpson's. They say she's very smart, she's got on a new bed-gown that her Cousin gave her, it's a very bonny one, they tell me, but I've not seen it. Sally and me's in luck." In the afternoon a poor woman came, *she said,* to beg some rags for her husband's leg, which had been

wounded by a slate from the roof in the great wind — but she has been used to go a-begging, for she has often come here. Her father lived to the age of 105. She is a woman of strong bones, with a complexion that has been beautiful, and remained very fresh last year, but now she looks broken, and her little boy — a pretty little fellow, and whom I have loved for the sake of Basil — looks thin and pale. I observed this to her. "Ay," says she, "we have all been ill. Our house was unroofed in the storm nearly, and so we lived in it so for more than a week." The child wears a ragged drab coat and a fur cap, poor little fellow, I think he seems scarcely at all grown since the first time I saw him. William was with me; we met him in a lane going to Skelwith Bridge. He looked very pretty. He was walking lazily, in the deep narrow lane, overshadowed with the hedgerows, his meal poke hung over his shoulder. He said he "was going a laiting". Poor creatures! He now wears the same coat he had on at that time. When the woman was gone, I could not help thinking that we are not half thankful enough that we are placed in that condition of life in which we are. We do not so often bless God for this, as we wish for this £50, that £100, etc. etc. We have not, however, to reproach ourselves with ever breathing a murmur. This woman's was but a *common* case. The snow still lies upon the ground. Just at the closing in of the day, I heard a cart pass the door, and at the same time the dismal sound of a crying infant. I went to the window, and had light enough to see that a man was driving a cart, which seemed not to be very full, and that a woman with an infant in her arms was following close behind and a dog close to her. It was a wild and melancholy sight. Wm. rubbed his table after candles were lighted, and we sate a long time with the windows unclosed; I almost finished writing *The Pedlar*; but poor Wm. wore himself and me out with labour. We had an affecting conversation. Went to bed at 12 o'clock.

February 13th, Saturday. It snowed a little this morning. Still at work at *The Pedlar,* altering and refitting. We did not walk, though it was a very fine day. We received a present of eggs and milk from Janet Dockeray, and just before she went, the little boy from the Hill brought us a letter from Sara H., and one from the Frenchman in London. I wrote to Sara after tea, and Wm. took out his old newspapers, and the new ones came in soon after. We sate, after I had finished the letter, talking; and Wm. read parts of his *Recluse* aloud to me. We did not drink tea till ½ past 7.

February 14th, Sunday. A fine morning. The sun shines but it has been a hard frost in the night. There are some little snowdrops that are afraid to pop their white heads quite out, and a few blossoms of Hepatica that are half-starved. Wm. left me at work altering some passages of *The Pedlar,* and went into the orchard. The fine day pushed him on to resolve; and as soon as I had read a letter to him, which I had just received from Mrs. Clarkson, he said he would go to Penrith, so Molly was despatched for the horse. I worked hard, got the backs pasted, the writing finished, and all quite trim. I wrote to Mrs. Clarkson, and put up some letters for Mary H., and off he went in his blue spencer, and a pair of *new* pantaloons fresh from London. He turned back when he had got as far as Frank's to ask if he had his letters safe, then for some apples, then fairly off. We had money to borrow for him. It was a pleasant afternoon. I ate a little bit of cold mutton without laying cloth and then sate over the fire, reading Ben Jonson's *Penshurst,* and other things. Before sunset I put on my shawl and walked out. The snow-covered mountains were spotted with rich sunlight, a palish buffish colour. The roads were very dirty for, though it was a keen frost, the sun had melted the snow and water upon them. I stood at Sara's gate, and when I came in view of Rydale, I cast a long look upon the mountains beyond. They were very white, but I concluded that Wm. would have a very safe passage over Kirkstone, and I was quite easy about him. After dinner, a little before sunset, I walked out about 20 yards above Glow-worm Rock. I met a carman, a Highlander I suppose, with 4 carts, the first 3 belonging to himself, the last evidently to a man and his family who had joined company with him, and who I guessed to be potters. The carman was cheering his horses, and talking to a little lass about 10 years of age who seemed to make him her companion. She ran to the wall, and took up a large stone to support the wheel of one of his carts, and ran on before with it in her

'. . . and a few blossoms of Hepatica.'

arms to be ready for him. She was a beautiful creature, and there was something uncommonly impressive in the lightness and joyousness of her manner. Her business seemed to be all pleasure — pleasure in her own motions, and the man looked at her as if he too was pleased, and spoke to her in the same tone in which he spoke to his horses. There was a wildness in her whole figure, not the wildness of a Mountain lass, but a *Road* lass, a traveller from her birth, who had wanted neither food nor clothes. Her Mother followed the last cart with a lovely child, perhaps about a year old, at her back, and a good-looking girl, about 15 years old, walked beside her. All the children were like the mother. She had a very fresh complexion, but she was blown with fagging up the hill, with the steepness of the hill and the bairn that she carried. Her husband was helping the horse to drag the cart up by pushing it with his shoulder. I got tea when I reached home, and read German till about 9 o'clock. Then Molly went away and I wrote to Coleridge. Went to bed at about 12 o'clock. Slept in Wm.'s bed and I slept badly, for my thoughts were full of William.

February 15th, *Monday.* I was starching small linen all the morning. It snowed a good deal, and was terribly cold. After dinner it was fair, but I was obliged to run all the way to the foot of the White Moss, to get the least bit of warmth into me. I found a letter from C. — he was much better — this was very satisfactory, but his letter was not an answer to Wm.'s which I expected. A letter from Annette. I got tea when I reached home, and then set on to reading German. I wrote part of a letter to Coleridge, went late to bed and slept badly.

[*February*] 16th, *Tuesday.* A fine morning, but I had persuaded myself not to expect Wm.; I believe because I was afraid of being disappointed. I ironed all day. He came in just at tea time, had only seen Mary H. for a couple of hours between Eamont Bridge and Hartshorn Tree. Mrs. C. better. He had had a difficult journey over Kirkstone, and came home by Threlkeld — his mouth and breath were very cold when he kissed me. We spent a sweet evening. He was better, had altered *The Pedlar.* We went to bed pretty soon. Mr. Graham said he wished Wm. had been with him the other day — he was riding in a post-chaise and he heard a strange cry that he could not understand, the sound continued, and he called to the chaise driver to stop. It was a little girl that was crying as if her heart would burst. She had got up behind the chaise, and her cloak had been caught by the wheel, and was jammed in, and it hung there. She was crying after it. Poor thing. Mr. Graham took her into the chaise, and the cloak was released from the wheel, but the child's misery did not cease, for her cloak was torn to rags; it had been a miserable cloak before, but she had no other, and it was the greatest sorrow that could befal her. Her name was Alice Fell. She had no parents, and belonged to the next town. At the next town, Mr. G. left money with some respectable people in the town, to buy her a new cloak.

[*February*] 17th, *Wednesday.* A miserable nasty snowy morning. We did not walk, but the old man from the hill brought us a short letter from Mary H. I copied the second part of *Peter Bell.* William pretty well.

[*February*] 18th, *Thursday.* A foggy morning, but it cleared up in the afternoon,

and Wm. went to Mrs. Simpson's to tea. I went with him to Goan Mackereth's. Roads very dirty. I copied third part of *Peter Bell* in his absence, and began a letter to Coleridge. Wm. came in with a letter from Coleridge, that came by Keswick. We talked together till 11 o'clock, when Wm. got to work, and was the worse for it. Hard frost.

[*February*] 19*th, Friday*. Hard frost this morning, but it soon snowed, then thawed — a miserable afternoon. Williamson came and cut William's hair — I wrote to C. He carried the letter to Ambleside. Afterwards I wrote to Mary and Sara, tired and went early to bed.

[*February*] 20*th, Saturday*. A very rainy morning, but it cleared up a little — we walked to Rydale, there were no letters. The roads were very dirty. We met little Dawson on horseback and desired him to bring us paper from Mrs. Jameson's. After tea I wrote the first part of *Peter Bell*. William better.

[*February*] 21*st, Sunday*. A very wet morning. I wrote the 2nd prologue to *Peter Bell,* then went to Mrs. Olliff's. After dinner I wrote the 1st prologue. William walked to the Tailor's, while I was at Mrs. O.'s — it rained all the time. Snowdrops quite out, but cold and winterly; yet, for all this, a thrush that lives in our orchard has shouted and sung its merriest all day long. In the evening I wrote to Mrs. Clarkson, and my Br. Richard. Wm. went to bed exhausted.

[*February*] 22*nd, Monday*. A wet morning. I lay down, as soon as breakfast was over, very unwell. I slept. Wm. brought me 4 letters to bed.— from Annette and Caroline, Mary and Sara, and Coleridge. C. had had another attack in his bowels; otherwise mending — M. and S. both well. M. reached Middleham the Monday night before at 12 o'clock — Tom there. In the evening we walked to the top of the hill, then to the bridge, we hung over the wall, and looked at the deep stream below; it came with a full, steady, yet very rapid flow down to the lake. The sykes made a sweet sound everywhere, and looked very interesting in the twilight. That little one above Mr. Olliff's house was very impressive. A ghostly white serpent line, it made a sound most distinctly heard of itself. The mountains were black and steep — the tops of some of them having yet snow visible, but it rained so hard last night much of it has been washed away. After tea I was just going to write to Coleridge when Mr. Simpson came in. Wm. began to read *Peter Bell* to him, so I carried my writing to the kitchen fire. Wm. called me upstairs to read the 3rd part. Mr. S. had brought his first engraving to let us see — he supped with us. Wm. was tired with reading and talking and went to bed in bad spirits.

[*February*] *23rd, Tuesday.* A misty rainy morning — the lake calm. I baked bread and pies. Before dinner worked a little at Wm.'s waistcoat — after dinner read German Grammar. Before tea we walked into Easedale. We turned aside in the Parson's field, a pretty field with 3 pretty prospects. Then we went to the first large field, but such a cold wind met us that we turn'd again. The wind seemed warm when we came out of our own door. That dear thrush was singing upon the topmost of the smooth branches of the ash tree at the top of the orchard. How long it had been perched on that same tree I cannot tell, but we had heard its dear voice in the orchard the day through, along with a chearful undersong made by

MISSEL-THRUSH.

View from Grange Bridge, Borrowdale, by John Varley

our winter friends, the robins. We came home by Goan's. I picked up a few mosses by the roadside, which I left at home. We then went to John's Grove, there we sate a little while looking at the fading landscape. The lake, though the objects on the shore were fading, seemed brighter than when it is perfect day, and the Island pushed itself upwards, distinct and large. All the shores marked. There was a sweet, sea-like sound in the trees above our heads. We walked backwards and forwards some time for dear John's sake, then walked to look at Rydale. Darkish when we reached home, and we got tea immediately with candles. William now reading in Bishop Hall — I going to read German. We have a nice singing fire, with one piece of wood. Fletcher's carts are arrived but no papers from Mrs. Coleridge.

[*February*] 24*th, Wednesday*. A rainy day — we were busy all day unripping William's coats for the tailor. William wrote to Annette, to Coleridge and the Frenchman — I received a letter from Mrs. Clarkson, a very kind affecting letter, which I answered telling her I would go to Eusemere when William went to Keswick — I wrote a little bit to Coleridge. We sent off these letters by Fletcher. It was a tremendous night of wind and rain. Poor Coleridge! a sad night for a traveller such as he. God be praised he was in safe quarters. Wm. went out, and put the letters under the door — he never felt a colder night.

[*February*] 25*th, Thursday*. A fine, mild, grey, beautiful morning. The tailor here. I worked at unripping. Wm. wrote to Montagu in the morning. After dinner he went to Lloyd's — I accompanied him to the gate in the corner or turning of the vale close to the riverside beyond Lenty Fleming's Cottage. It was coldish and like for frost — a clear evening. I reached home just before dark, brought some mosses and ivy, then got tea, and fell to work at German. I read a good deal of Lessing's Essay. Wm. came home between 9 and 10 o'clock. We sate nicely together by the fire till bedtime. Wm. not very much tired.

[*February*] 26th, *Friday*. A grey morning till 10 o'clock, then the sun shone beautifully. Mrs. Lloyd's children and Mrs. Luff came in a chaise, were here at 11 o'clock, then went to Mrs. Olliff. Wm. and I accompanied them to the gate. I prepared dinner, sought out *Peter Bell,* gave Wm. some cold meat, and then we went to walk. We walked first to Butterlip How, where we sate and overlooked the vale; no sign of spring but the red tints of the upper twigs of the woods and single trees. Sate in the sun. Met Charles Lloyd near the Bridge, got dinner — I lay down unwell — got up to tea. Mr. and Mrs. Luff walked home, the Lloyds stayed till 8 o'clock. We always get on better with conversation at home than elsewhere — discussion about Mrs. King and Mrs. Olliff. The chaise-driver brought us a letter from M. H., a short one from C. We were perplexed about Sara's coming. I wrote to Mary. Wm. closed his letter to Montagu, and wrote to Calvert and to Mrs. Coleridge. Birds sang divinely to-day. Bowels and head bad. Wm. better.

[*February*] 27th, *Saturday*. We walked in the afternoon towards Rydale returning to tea. Mr. Barth Simpson called after supper, a little tipsy. Fletcher said he had had no papers. Wm was not very well. I sate in the orchard after dinner — we walked in the evening towards Rydale.

February 28th, Sunday. Wm. very ill, employed with *The Pedlar*. We got papers in the morning. William shaved himself. I was obliged to go to bed after dinner, rose better — wrote to Sara H. and Mrs. Clarkson — no walk. Disaster Pedlar.

[*March 1st,*] *Monday*. A fine pleasant day, we walked to Rydale. I went on before for the letters, brought 2 from M. and S. H. We climbed over the wall and read them under the shelter of a mossy rock. We met Mrs. Lloyd in going — Mrs. Olliff's child ill. The catkins are beautiful in the hedges, the ivy is very green. Robert Newton's paddock is greenish — that is all we see of Spring; finished and sent off the letter to Sara, and wrote to Mary. Wrote again to Sara, and Wm. wrote to Coleridge. Mrs. Lloyd called when I was in bed.

[*March 2nd,*] *Tuesday*. A fine grey morning. I was baking bread and pies. After dinner I read German, and a little before dinner Wm. also read. We walked on Butterlip How under the wind. It rained all the while, but we had a pleasant walk. The mountains of Easedale, black or covered with snow at the tops, gave a peculiar softness to the valley, the clouds hid the tops of some of them. The valley was populous and enlivened with the streams. Mrs. Lloyd drove past without calling.

[*March 3rd,*] *Wednesday*. I was so unlucky as to propose to rewrite *The Pedlar*. Wm. got to work, and was worn to death. We did not walk. I wrote in the

Brummer Head, Easedale, by Thomas Austin

afternoon.

[*March 4th,*] *Thursday*. Before we had quite finished breakfast Calvert's man brought the horses for Wm. We had a deal to do, to shave, pens to make, poems to put in order for writing, to settle the dress, pack up etc., and the man came before the pens were made, and he was obliged to leave me with only two. Since he has left me at half-past 11 (it is now 2) I have been putting the drawers into order, laid by his clothes which we had thrown here and there and everywhere, filed two months' newspapers and got my dinner, 2 boiled eggs and 2 apple tarts. I have set Molly on to clear the garden a little, and I myself have helped. I transplanted some snowdrops — the Bees are busy. Wm. has a nice bright day. It was hard frost in the night. The Robins are singing sweetly. Now for my walk. I *will* be busy. I *will* look well, and be well when he comes back to me. O the Darling! Here is one of his bitten apples. I can hardly find it in my heart to throw it into the fire. I must wash myself, then off. I walked round the two Lakes, crossed the stepping-stones at Rydale foot. Sate down where we always sit. I was full of thoughts about my darling. Blessings on him. I came home at the foot of our own hill under Loughrigg. They are making sad ravages in the woods. Benson's wood is going, and the wood above the River. The wind has blown down a small fir tree on the Rock that terminates John's path — I suppose the wind of Wednesday night. I read German after my return till tea time. I worked

The Village Doctress,
by John Harden

P.5

and read the L. B., enchanted with the *Idiot Boy*. Wrote to Wm., then went to bed. It snowed when I went to bed.

[*March 5th,*] *Friday*. First walked in the garden and orchard, a frosty sunny morning. After dinner I gathered mosses in Easedale. I saw before me sitting in the open field upon his sack of rags the old Ragman that I know. His coat is of scarlet in a thousand patches. His breeches' knees were untied. The breeches have been given him by some one — he has a round hat, pretty good, small crowned but large rimmed. When I came to him, he said "Is there a brigg yonder that'll carry me ow'r t'watter?" He seemed half stupid. When I came home Molly had shook the carpet and cleaned everything upstairs. When I see her so happy in her work, and exulting in her own importance, I often think of that affecting expression which she made use of to me one evening lately. Talking of her good luck in being in this house, "Aye, Mistress, them 'at's low laid would have been a proud creature could they but have [seen] where I is now, fra what they thought mud be my doom". I was tired when I reached home. I sent Molly Ashburner to Rydale. No letters! I was sadly mortified. I expected one fully from Coleridge. Wrote to William, read the L. B., got into sad thoughts, tried at German, but could not go on. Read L. B. Blessings on that Brother of mine! Beautiful new moon over Silver How.

[*March 6th,*] *Saturday Morning*. I awoke with a bad headache and partly on that account, partly for ease I lay in bed till one o'clock. At one I pulled off my nightcap — ½ past one sate down to breakfast. A very cold sunshiny frost. I wrote *The Pedlar,* and finished it before I went to Mr. Simpson's to drink tea. Miss S. at Keswick, but she came home. Mrs. Jameson came in — I stayed supper. Fletcher's carts went past and I let them go with William's letter. Mr. B. S. came nearly home with me. I found letters from Wm., Mary, and Coleridge. I wrote to C. Sate up late, and could not fall asleep when I went to bed.

[*March 7th,*] *Sunday Morning*. A very fine, clear frost. I stitched up *The Pedlar;* wrote out *Ruth;* read it with the alterations; then wrote to Mary H. Read a little German, got my dinner. Mrs. Lloyd called at the door, and in came William. I did not expect him till to-morrow. How glad I was. After we had talked about an hour, I gave him his dinner, a beef steak. We sate talking and happy. Mr. and Miss Simpson came in at tea time. William came home very well — he had been a little fatigued with reading his poems. He brought two new stanzas of *Ruth*. We went to bed pretty soon and slept well. A mild grey evening.

[*March 8th,*] *Monday Morning*. A soft rain and mist. We walked to Rydale for letters. The Vale looked very beautiful in excessive simplicity, yet, at the same time, in uncommon obscurity. The Church stood alone, no mountains behind. The meadows looked calm and rich, bordering on the still lake. Nothing else to be seen but lake and island. Found a very affecting letter from Montagu, also one from Mary. We read Montagu's in walking on — sate down to read Mary's. I came home with a bad headach and lay down — I slept, but rose little better. I have got tea and am now much relieved. On Friday evening the moon hung over the northern side of the highest point of Silver How, like a gold ring snapped in two, and shaven off at the ends, it was so narrow. Within this ring lay the circle of the round moon, as *distinctly* to be seen as ever the enlightened moon is. William had observed the same appearance at Keswick, perhaps at the very same moment, hanging over the Newland Fells. Sent off a letter to Mary H., also to Coleridge and Sara, and rewrote in the evening the alterations of *Ruth,* which we sent off at the same time.

[*March 9th,*] *Tuesday Morning*. William was reading in Ben Jonson — he read me a beautiful poem on Love. We then walked. The first part of our walk was melancholy — we went within view of Rydale — then we sate on Sara's seat — we walked afterwards into Easedale. It was cold when we returned. We met Sally Newton and her water dog. We sate by the fire in the evening, and read *The Pedlar* over. William worked a little, and altered it in a few places. I was not very well — mended stockings.

[*March 10th,*] *Wednesday*. A fine mildish morning, that is, not frost. Wm. read in Ben Jonson in the morning. I read a little German, altered various waistcoats. We then walked to Rydale. No letters! They are slashing away in Benson's wood. We walked round by the Church, through Olliff's field when we returned, then home and went up into the orchard. We sate on the seat, talked a little by the fire and then got our tea. William has since tea been talking about publishing the

Woodmen, by W. H. Pyne

Yorkshire Wolds Poem with *The Pedlar.*

[*March* 11*th,*] *Thursday.* A fine morning. William worked at the poem of *The Singing Bird.* Just as we were sitting down to dinner we heard Mr. Clarkson's voice. I ran down, William followed. He was so finely mounted that William was more intent upon the horse than the rider, an offence easily forgiven, for Mr. Clarkson was as proud of it himself as he well could be. We ate our dinner, then Mr. Clarkson came. We walked with him round by the White Bridge after dinner. The vale in mist, rather the mountains, big with the rain, soft and beautiful. Mr. C. was sleepy and went soon to bed.

[*March* 12*th,*] *Friday.* A very fine morning. We went to see Mr. Clarkson off. Then we went up towards Easedale but a shower drove us back. The sun shone while it rained, and the stones of the walls and the pebbles on the road glittered like silver. When William was at Keswick I saw Jane Ashburner driving the cow along the high road from the well where she had been watering it — she had a stick in her hand and came tripping along in the jig-step, as if she were dancing. Her presence was bold and graceful, her cheeks flushed with health, and her countenance was free and gay. William finished his poem of *The Singing Bird.* In the meantime I read the remainder of Lessing. In the evening after tea William wrote *Alice Fell* — he went to bed tired, with a wakeful mind and a weary body. A very sharp clear night.

[*March* 13*th,*] *Saturday Morning.* It was as cold as ever it has been all winter, very hard frost. I baked pies bread and seed cake for Mr. Simpson. William finished *Alice Fell,* and then he wrote the poem of *The Beggar Woman,* taken from a woman whom I had seen in May (now nearly 2 years ago) when John and he were at Gallow Hill. I sate with him at intervals all the morning, took down his stanzas, etc. After dinner we walked to Rydale for letters — it was terribly cold — we had 2 or 3 brisk hail showers — the hail stones looked clean and pretty upon the dry clean road. Little Peggy Simpson was standing at the door catching the hail stones in her hand — she grows very like her mother. When she is sixteen years old I dare say that to her Grandmother's eye she will seem as like to what her mother was, as any rose in her garden is like the rose that grew there years before. No letters at Rydale. We drank tea as soon as we reached home. After tea I read to William that account of the little boy belonging to the tall woman, and an unlucky thing it was, for he could not escape from those very words, and so he could not write the poem. He left it unfinished, and went tired to bed. In our walk from Rydale he had got warmed with the subject, and had half cast the poem.

[*March* 14*th,*] *Sunday Morning.* William had slept badly — he got up at nine o'clock, but before he rose he had finished *The Beggar Boys,* and while we were at breakfast that is (for I had breakfasted) he, with his basin of broth before him untouched, and a little plate of bread and butter he wrote the Poem to a Butterfly! He ate not a morsel, nor put on his stockings, but sate with his shirt neck unbuttoned, and his waistcoat open while he did it. The thought first came upon him as we were talking about the pleasure we both always feel at the sight of a butterfly. I told him that I used to chase them a little, but that I was afraid of brushing the dust off their wings, and did not catch them. He told me how they used to kill all the white ones when he went to school because they were Frenchmen. Mr. Simpson came in just as he was finishing the Poem. After he was gone I wrote it down and the other poems, and I read them all over to him. We then called at Mr. Olliff's — Mr. O. walked with us to within sight of Rydale — the sun shone very pleasantly, yet it was extremely cold. We dined and then Wm. went to bed. I lay upon the fur gown before the fire, but I could not sleep — I lay there a long time. It is now halfpast 5 — I am going to write letters — I began to write to Mrs. Rawson. William rose without having slept — we sate comfortably by the fire till he began to try to alter *The Butterfly,* and tired himself — he went to bed tired.

[*March 15th,*] *Monday Morning.* We sate reading the poems, and I read a little German. Mr. Luff came in at one o'clock. He had a long talk with William — he went to Mr. Olliff's after dinner and returned to us to tea. During his absence a sailor who was travelling from Liverpool to Whitehaven called; he was faint and

Scullery Maid, by John Harden

TO A BUTTERFLY

Stay near me — do not take thy flight!
A little longer stay in sight!
Much converse do I find in thee,
Historian of my infancy!
Float near me; do not yet depart!
Dead times revive in thee:
Thou bring'st, gay creature as thou art!
A solemn image to my heart,
My father's family!

Oh! pleasant, pleasant were the days,
The time, when, in our childish plays,
My sister Emmeline and I
Together chased the butterfly!
A very hunter did I rush
Upon the prey: — with leaps and springs
I followed on from brake to bush;
But she, God love her! feared to brush
The dust from off its wings.

William Wordsworth

pale when he knocked at the door — a young man very well dressed. We sate by the kitchen fire talking with him for 2 hours. He told us interesting stories of his life. His name was Isaac Chapel. He had been at sea since he was 15 years old. He was by trade a sail-maker. His last voyage was to the coast of Guinea. He had been on board a slave ship, the captain's name Maxwell, where one man had been killed, a boy put to lodge with the pigs and was half eaten, one boy set to watch in the hot sun till he dropped down dead. He had been cast away in North America and had travelled thirty days among the Indians, where he had been well treated. He had twice swum from a King's ship in the night and escaped. He said he would rather be in hell than be pressed. He was now going to wait in England to appear against Captain Maxwell. "O he's a Rascal, Sir, he ought to be put in the papers!" The poor man had not been in bed since Friday night. He left Liverpool at 2 o'clock on Saturday morning; he had called at a farm house to beg victuals and had been refused. The woman said she would give him nothing. "Won't you? Then I can't help it." He was excessively like my brother John. A letter was brought us at tea time by John Dawson from M. H. I wrote to her, to Sara about Mr. Olliff's gig, and to Longman and Rees — I wrote to Mrs. Clarkson by Mr. Luff.

[*March 16th,*] *Tuesday.* A very fine morning. Mrs. Luff called — William went up into the orchard while she was here and wrote a part of *The Emigrant Mother.* After dinner I read him to sleep. I read Spenser while he leaned upon my shoulder. We walked to look at Rydale. Then we walked towards Goan's. The moon was a good height above the mountains. She seemed far and distant in the sky; there were two stars beside her, that twinkled in and out, and seemed almost like butterflies in motion and lightness. They looked to be far nearer to us than the moon.

[*March 17th,*] *Wednesday.* William went up into the orchard and finished the Poem. Mrs. Luff and Mrs. Olliff called. I went with Mrs. O. to the top of the White Moss — Mr. O. met us and I went to their house — he offered me manure for the garden. I went and sate with W. and walked backwards and forwards in the orchard till dinner time. He read me his poem. I broiled beefsteaks. After dinner we made a pillow of my shoulder — I read to him and my Beloved slept. I afterwards got him the pillows, and he was lying with his head on the table when Miss Simpson came in. She stayed tea. I went with her to Rydale — no letters! A sweet evening as it had been a sweet day, a grey evening, and I walked quietly along the side of Rydale Lake with quiet thoughts — the hills and the lake were still — the Owls had not begun to hoot, and the little birds had given over singing. I looked before me and I saw a red light upon Silver How as if coming out of the vale below,

> *There was a light of most strange birth,*
> *A light that came out of the earth,*
> *And spread along the dark hill-side.*

Thus I was going on when I saw the shape of my Beloved in the road at a little distance. We turned back to see the light but it was fading — almost gone. The owls hooted when we sate on the wall at the foot of White Moss; the sky broke more and more, and we saw the moon now and then. John Green passed us with his cart — we sate on. When we came in sight of our own dear Grasmere, the vale looked fair and quiet in the moonshine, the Church was there and all the cottages. There were huge slow-travelling clouds in the sky, that threw large masses of shade upon some of the mountains. We walked backwards and forwards, between home and Olliff's, till I was tired. William kindled, and began to write the poem. We carried cloaks into the orchard, and sate a while there. I left him, and he nearly finished the poem. I was tired to death, and went to bed before him — he came down to me, and read the poem to me in bed. A sailor begged here to-day, going to Glasgow. He spoke chearfully in a sweet tone.

[*March 18th,*] *Thursday.* A very fine morning. The sun shone, but it was far colder than yesterday. I felt myself weak and William charged me not to go to Mrs. Lloyd's. I seemed indeed to myself unfit for it, but when he was gone I thought I would get the visit over if I could, so I ate a beefsteak thinking it would strengthen me; so it did, and I went off. I had a very pleasant walk — Rydale vale was full of life and motion. The wind blew briskly, and the lake was covered all over with bright silver waves, that were there each the twinkling of an eye, then others rose up and took their place as fast as they went away. The rocks glittered in the sunshine, the crows and the ravens were busy, and the thrushes and little birds sang. I went through the fields, and sate ½ an hour afraid to pass a cow. The cow looked at me, and I looked at the cow, and whenever I stirred the cow gave over eating. I was not very much tired when I reached Lloyd's — I walked in the garden — Charles is all for agriculture — Mrs. L. in her kindest way. A parcel came in from Birmingham, with Lamb's play for us, and for C. They came with me as far as Rydale. As we came along Ambleside vale in the twilight it was a grave evening. There was something in the air that compelled me to serious thought — the hills were large, closed in by the sky. It was nearly dark when I parted from the Lloyds, that is night was come on, and the moon was overcast. But, as I climbed Moss, the moon came out from behind a mountain mass of black clouds. O, the unutterable darkness of the sky, and the earth below the moon! and the glorious brightness of the moon itself! There was a vivid sparkling streak of light at this end of Rydale water, but the rest was very dark, and Loughrigg Fell and Silver How were white and bright, as if they were covered with hoar frost. The moon retired again, and appeared and disappeared several times before I reached home. Once there was no moonlight to be seen but upon the island-house and the promontory of the island where it stands. "That needs must be a holy place", etc. etc. I had many very exquisite feelings, and when I saw this lowly Building in the waters, among the dark and lofty hills, with that bright, soft light upon it, it made me more than half a poet. I was tired when I reached home, and could not sit down to reading, and tried to write verses, but alas! I gave up expecting William, and went soon to bed. Fletcher's carts came home late.

Anemone (eighteenth-century embroidery)

Portinscale Bridge, by William Westall

[*March 19th,*] *Friday.* A very rainy morning. I went up into the lane to collect a few green mosses to make the chimney gay against my darling's return. Poor C., I did not wish for, or expect him, it rained so. Mr. Luff came in before my dinner. We had a long talk. He left me before 4 o'clock, and about half an hour after Coleridge came in — his eyes were a little swollen with the wind. I was much affected with the sight of him, he seemed half stupefied. William came in soon after. Coleridge went to bed late, and William and I sate up till four o'clock. A letter from Sara sent by Mary. They disputed about Ben Jonson. My spirits were agitated very much.

[*March 20th,*] *Saturday.* A tolerably fine morning after 11 o'clock but when I awoke the whole vale was covered with snow. William and Coleridge walked to Borwick's. I followed but did not find them — came home and they were here. We had a little talk about going abroad. We sate pleasantly enough. After tea William read *The Pedlar.* After supper we talked about various things — christening the children, etc. etc. Went to bed at 12 o'clock.

[*March 21st,*] *Sunday.* A showery day. Coleridge and William lay long in bed. We sent up to Mackareth's for the horse to go to Keswick, but we could not have it. Went with C. to Borwick's where he left us. William was very unwell this evening. We had a sweet and tender conversation. I wrote to Mary and Sara.

[*March 22nd,*] *Monday.* A rainy day. William very poorly. Mr. Luff came in after dinner and brought us 2 letters from Sara H. and one from poor Annette. I read Sara's letters while he was here, I finished my letters to M. and S. and wrote to my brother Richard. We talked a good deal about C. and other interesting things. We resolved to see Annette, and that Wm. should go to Mary. Wm. wrote to Coleridge not to expect us till Thursday or Friday.

[*March 23rd,*] *Tuesday.* A mild morning. William worked at *The Cuckow* poem. I sewed beside him. After dinner he slept, I read German, and, at the closing-in of day, went to sit in the orchard — he came to me, and walked backwards and forwards. We talked about C. Wm. repeated the poem to me. I left him there, and in 20 minutes he came in, rather tired with attempting to write. He is now reading Ben Jonson. I am going to read German. It is about 10 o'clock, a quiet night. The fire flutters, and the watch ticks. I hear nothing else save the breathing of my Beloved, and he now and then pushes his book forward, and turns over a leaf. Fletcher is not come home. No letter from C.

[*March 24th,*] *Wednesday.* We walked to Rydale for letters. It was a beautiful spring morning — warm, and quiet with mists. We found a letter from M. H. I made a vow that we would not leave this country for G. Hill[1] — Sara and Tom not being going to the Wolds. I wrote to Mary in the evening. I went to bed after dinner. William walked out and wrote [to] Peggy Ashburner — I rose better. Wm. altered *The Butterfly* as we came from Rydale.

1. Gallow Hill, Yorkshire, where the Hutchinsons were then farming.

[*March 25th,*] *Thursday.* We did not walk though it was a fine day — [? old] Mrs. Simpson drank tea with us. No letter from Coleridge.

[*March 26th,*] *Friday.* A beautiful morning. William wrote to Annette, then

TO THE CUCKOO

O blithe New-comer! I have heard,
I hear thee and rejoice.
O Cuckoo! shall I call thee Bird,
Or but a wandering Voice?

While I am lying on the grass
Thy twofold shout I hear,
From hill to hill it seems to pass
At once far off, and near.

Though babbling only to the Vale,
Of sunshine and of flowers,
Thou bringest unto me a tale
Of visionary hours.

Thrice welcome, darling of the Spring!
Even yet thou art to me
No bird, but an invisible thing,
A voice, a mystery;

The same whom in my schoolboy days
I listened to; that Cry
Which made me look a thousand ways
In bush, and tree, and sky.

To seek thee did I often rove
Through woods and on the green;
And thou wert still a hope, a love;
Still longed for, never seen.

And I can listen to thee yet;
Can lie upon the plain
And listen, till I do beget
That golden time again.

O Blessèd Bird! the earth we pace
Again appears to be
An unsubstantial, faery place;
That is fit home for Thee!

William Wordsworth

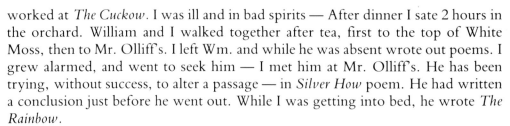
worked at *The Cuckow*. I was ill and in bad spirits — After dinner I sate 2 hours in the orchard. William and I walked together after tea, first to the top of White Moss, then to Mr. Olliff's. I left Wm. and while he was absent wrote out poems. I grew alarmed, and went to seek him — I met him at Mr. Olliff's. He has been trying, without success, to alter a passage — in *Silver How* poem. He had written a conclusion just before he went out. While I was getting into bed, he wrote *The Rainbow*.

[*March 27th,*] *Saturday*. A divine morning. At breakfast William wrote part of an ode. Mr. Olliff sent the dung and Wm. went to work in the garden. We sate all day in the orchard.

[*March 28th,*] *Sunday*. We went to Keswick. Arrived wet to skin. A letter from Mary. C. was not tired with walking to meet us. I lay down after dinner with a bad headach.

[*March 29th,*] *Monday*. A cold day. I went down to Miss Crosthwaite's to unpack the box — Wm. and C. went to Armathwaite — a letter from S. H. — had headach, I lay till after tea. Conversation with Mrs. Coleridge.

March 30th, Tuesday. We went to Calvert's. I was somewhat better though not well.

March 31st, Wednesday. Very unwell. We walked to Portinscale, lay upon the turf, and saw into the Vale of Newlands up to Borrowdale, and down to Keswick — a soft Venetian view. I returned better. Calvert and Wilkinsons dined with us. I walked with Mrs. W. to the Quaker's meeting, met Wm., and we walked in the field together.

April 1st, Thursday. Mrs. C., Wm., C. and I went to the How — a pleasant morning. We came home by Portinscale — sate for some time on the hill.

[*April*] *2nd, Friday*. Wm. and I sate all the morning in the field. I nursed Derwent. Drank tea with the Miss Cockins.

[*April*] *3rd, Saturday*. Wm. went on to Skiddaw with C. we dined at Calvert's. Fine day.

[*April*] *4th, Sunday*. We drove in the gig to Water End — I walked down to Coleridge's. Mrs. C.[1] came to Greta Bank to tea. Wm. walked down with Mrs. C. I repeated his verses to them. We sate pleasant-ly enough after supper.   1. *i.e.* Mrs. Calvert.

[*April*] *5th, Monday*. We came to Eusemere. Coleridge walked with us to Threlkeld—reached Eusemere to tea. The schoolmistress at Dacre and her scholars. Mrs. C. at work in the garden — she met us.

April 6th, Tuesday. Mrs. C., Wm. and I walked to Waterside. Wm. and I walked together in the evening towards Dalemain — the moon and stars.

[*April*] *7th, Wednesday*. Wm.'s birthday. Wm. went to Middleham. I walked 6 miles with him. It rained a little, but a fine day. Broth to supper, and went soon to bed.

[*April*] *8th, Thursday*. Mrs. C. and I walked to Woodside. We slept after dinner on the sofa — sate up till ½ past 10. Mrs. C. tired. I wrote to M. H. in the morning, to Sara in the evening.

Landscape with a Rainbow, by Joseph Wright

THE RAINBOW
(*Published as* My heart leaps up when I behold)

My heart leaps up when I behold
A rainbow in the sky:
So was it when my life began;
So is it now I am a man;
So be it when I shall grow old,
Or let me die!
The Child is father of the Man;
And I could wish my days to be
Bound each to each by natural piety.

William Wordsworth

[*April*] 9*th, Friday.* Mrs. C. planting. Sent off letters. A windy morning — rough lake — sun shines — very cold — a windy night. Walked in Dunmallet, marked our names on a tree.

[*April*] 10*th, Saturday.* Very cold — a stormy night, wrote to C. A letter from Wm. and S. H.

[*April*] 11*th, Sunday.* Very stormy and cold. I did not walk.

[*April*] 12*th, Monday.* Had the mantua-maker. The ground covered with snow. Walked to T. Wilkinson's and sent for letters. The woman brought me one from William and Mary. It was a sharp, windy night. Thomas Wilkinson came with me to Barton, and questioned me like a catechizer all the way. Every question was like the snapping of a little thread about my heart — I was so full of thought of my half-read letter and other things. I was glad when he left me. Then I had time to look at the moon while I was thinking over my own thoughts. The moon travelled through the clouds, tinging them yellow as she passed along, with two stars near her, one larger than the other. These stars grew or diminished as they passed from, or went into, the clouds. At this time William, as I found the next day, was riding by himself between Middleham and Barnard Castle, having parted from Mary. I read over my letter when I got to the house. Mr. and Mrs. C. were playing at cards.

April 13*th, Tuesday.* I had slept ill and was not well and obliged to go to bed in the afternoon — Mrs. C. waked me from sleep with a letter from Coleridge. After tea I went down to see the bank and walked along the Lakeside to the field where Mr. Smith thought of building his house. The air was become still, the lake

was of a bright slate colour, the hills darkening. The bays shot into the low fading shores. Sheep resting. All things quiet. When I returned Jane met me — *William* was come. The surprise shot through me. He looked well, but he was tired and went soon to bed after a dish of tea.

April 14*th, Wednesday*. William did not rise till dinner time. I walked with Mrs. C. I was ill, out of spirits, disheartened. Wm. and I took a long walk in the rain.

[*April*] 15*th, Thursday*. It was a threatening, misty morning, but mild. We set off after dinner from Eusemere. Mrs. Clarkson went a short way with us, but turned back. The wind was furious, and we thought we must have returned. We first rested in the large boat-house, then under a furze bush opposite Mr. Clarkson's. Saw the plough going in the field. The wind seized our breath. The Lake was rough. There was a boat by itself floating in the middle of the bay below Water Millock. We rested again in the Water Millock Lane. The hawthorns are black and green, the birches here and there greenish, but there is yet more of purple to be seen on the twigs. We got over into a field to avoid some cows — people working. A few primroses by the roadside — woodsorrel flower, the anemone, scentless violets, strawberries, and that starry, yellow flower which Mrs. C. calls pile wort. When we were in the woods beyond Gowbarrow Park we saw a few daffodils close to the water-side. We fancied that the lake had floated the seeds ashore, and that the little colony had so sprung up. But as we went along there were more and yet more; and at last, under the boughs of the trees, we saw that there was a long belt of them along the shore, about the breadth of a country turnpike road. I never saw daffodils so beautiful. They grew among

the mossy stones about and about them; some rested their heads upon these stones as on a pillow for weariness; and the rest tossed and reeled and danced, and seemed as if they verily laughed with the wind, that blew upon them over the lake; they looked so gay, ever glancing, ever changing. This wind blew directly over the lake to them. There was here and there a little knot, and a few stragglers a few yards higher up; but they were so few as not to disturb the simplicity, unity, and life of that one busy highway. We rested again and again. The bays were stormy, and we heard the waves at different distances, and in the middle of the water, like the sea. Rain came on — we were wet when we reached Luff's, but we called in. Luckily all was chearless and gloomy, so we faced the storm — we *must* have been wet if we had waited — put on dry clothes at Dobson's. I was very kindly treated by a young woman, the landlady looked sour, but it is her way. She gave us a goodish supper, excellent ham and potatoes. We paid 7/- when we came away. William was sitting by a bright fire when I came downstairs. He soon made his way to the library, piled up in a corner of the window. He brought out a volume of Enfield's *Speaker,* another miscellany, and an odd volume of Congreve's plays. We had a glass of warm rum and water. We enjoyed ourselves, and wished for Mary. It rained and blew, when we went to bed. N.B. Deer in Gowbarrow Park like skeletons.

April 16th, Friday (Good Friday). When I undrew my curtains in the morning, I was much affected by the beauty of the prospect, and the change. The sun shone, the wind had passed away, the hills looked chearful, the river was very bright as it flowed into the lake. The church rises up behind a little knot of rocks, the steeple not so high as an ordinary three-story house. Trees in a row in the garden under the wall. After Wm. had shaved we set forward; the valley is at first broken by little rocky woody knolls that make retiring places, fairy valleys in the vale; the river winds along under these hills, travelling, not in a bustle but not slowly, to the lake. We saw a fisherman in the flat meadow on the other side of the water. He came towards us, and threw his line over the two-arched bridge. It is a bridge of a heavy construction, almost bending inwards in the middle, but it is grey, and there is a look of ancientry in the architecture of it that pleased me. As we go on the vale opens out more into one vale, with somewhat of a cradle bed. Cottages, with groups of trees, on the side of the hills. We passed a pair of twin Children, 2 years old. Sate on the next bridge which we crossed — a single arch. We rested again upon the turf, and looked at the same bridge. We observed arches in the water, occasioned by the large stones sending it down in two streams. A sheep came plunging through the river, stumbled up the bank, and passed close to us, it had been frightened by an insignificant little dog on the other side, its fleece dropped a glittering shower under its belly. Primroses by the road-side, pile wort that shone like stars of gold in the sun, violets, strawberries, retired and half-buried among the grass. When we came to the foot of Brothers Water, I left William sitting on the bridge, and went along the path on the right side of the Lake through the wood. I was delighted with what I saw. The water under the boughs of the bare old trees, the simplicity of the mountains, and the exquisite

Ullswater from the Foot of Gowbarrow Fell, by J. C. Ibbetson

I WANDERED LONELY AS A CLOUD

I wandered lonely as a cloud
That floats on high o'er vales and hills,
When all at once I saw a crowd,
A host, of golden daffodils;
Beside the lake, beneath the trees,
Fluttering and dancing in the breeze.

Continuous as the stars that shine
And twinkle on the milky way,
They stretched in never-ending line
Along the margin of a bay;
Ten thousand saw I at a glance,
Tossing their heads in sprightly dance.

The waves beside them danced; but they
Out-did the sparkling waves in glee:
A poet could not but be gay,
In such a jocund company:
I gazed — and gazed — but little thought
What wealth the show to me had brought:

For oft, when on my couch I lie
In vacant or in pensive mood,
They flash upon that inward eye
Which is the bliss of solitude;
And then my heart with pleasure fills,
And dances with the daffodils.

William Wordsworth

beauty of the path. There was one grey cottage. I repeated *The Glow-worm,* as I walked along. I hung over the gate, and thought I could have stayed for ever. When I returned, I found William writing a poem descriptive of the sights and sounds we saw and heard. There was the gentle flowing of the stream, the glittering, lively lake, green fields without a living creature to be seen on them, behind us, a flat pasture with 42 cattle feeding; to our left, the road leading to the hamlet. No smoke there, the sun shone on the bare roofs. The people were at work ploughing, harrowing, and sowing; lasses spreading dung, a dog's barking now and then, cocks crowing, birds twittering, the snow in patches at the top of the highest hills, yellow palms, purple and green twigs on the birches, ashes with their glittering spikes quite bare. The hawthorn a bright green, with black stems under the oak. The moss of the oak glossy. We then went on, passed two sisters at work *(they first passed us),* one with two pitchforks in her hand, the other had a spade. We had some talk with them. They laughed aloud after we were gone, perhaps half in wantonness, half boldness. William finished his poem before we got to the foot of Kirkstone. There we ate our dinner. There were hundreds of cattle in the vale. The walk up Kirkstone was very interesting. The becks among the rocks were all alive. Wm. showed me the little mossy streamlet which he had before loved when he saw its bright green track in the snow. The view above Ambleside very beautiful. There we sate and looked down on the green vale. We watched the crows at a little distance from us become white as silver as they flew in the sunshine, and when they went still further, they looked like shapes of water passing over the green fields. The whitening of Ambleside church is a great deduction from the beauty of it, seen from this point. We called at the Luffs, the Boddingtons there. Did not go in, and went round by the fields. I pulled off my stockings, intending to wade the beck, but I was obliged to put them on, and we

climbed over the wall at the bridge. The post passed us. No letters! Rydale Lake was in its own evening brightness: the Islands and Points distinct. Jane Ashburner came up to us when we were sitting upon the wall. We rode in her cart to Tom Dawson's. All well. The garden looked pretty in the half-moonlight, half-daylight. As we went up the vale of Brother's Water more and more cattle feeding, 100 of them.

April 17th, Saturday. A mild warm rain. We sate in the garden all the morning. William dug a little. I transplanted a honey-suckle. The lake was still. The sheep on the island, reflected in the water, like the grey deer we saw in Gowbarrow Park. We walked after tea by moonlight. I had been in bed in the afternoon, and William had slept in his chair. We walked towards Rydale first, then backwards and forwards below Mr. Olliff's. The village was beautiful in the moonlight. Helm Crag we observed very distinct. The dead hedge round Benson's field bound together at the top by an interlacing of ash sticks, which made a chain of silver when we faced the moon. A letter from C. and also from S. H. I saw a robin chacing a scarlet butterfly this morning.

[*April*] *18th, Sunday*. I lay in bed late, again a mild grey morning, with rising vapours. We sate in the orchard. William wrote the poem on *The Robin and the Butterfly*. I went to drink tea at Luff's, but as we did not dine till 6 o'clock it was late. It was mist and small rain all the way, but very pleasant. William met me at Rydale — Aggie accompanied me thither. We sate up late. He met me with the conclusion of the poem of the Robin. I read it to him in bed. We left out some lines.

[*April*] *19th, Monday*. A mild rain, very warm. Wm. worked in the garden — I made pies and bread. After dinner the mist cleared away and sun shone. Wm. walked to Luff's — I was not very well and went to bed. Wm. came home pale and tired. I could not rest when I got to bed.

April 20th, Tuesday. A beautiful morning. The sun shone. William wrote a conclusion to the poem of the Butterfly — "I've watched you now a full half-hour". I was quite out of spirits, and went into the orchard. When I came in, he had finished the poem. We sate in the orchard after dinner — it was a beautiful afternoon. The sun shone upon the level fields, and they grew greener beneath the eye. Houses, village, all chearful — people at work. We sate in the orchard and repeated *The Glow-worm* and other poems. Just when William came to a well or a trough, which there is in Lord Darlington's park, he began to write that poem of *The Glow-worm,* not being able to ride upon the long trot — interrupted in going through the town of Staindrop, finished it about 2 miles and a half beyond Staindrop. He did not feel the jogging of the horse while he was writing; but, when he had done, he felt the effect of it, and his fingers were cold with his gloves. His horse fell with him on the other side of St. Helen's, Auckland. So much for *The Glow-worm*. It was written coming from Middleham on Monday, 12th April 1802. On Tuesday 20th, when we were sitting after tea, Coleridge came to the door. I startled Wm. with my voice. C. came up palish, but I afterwards found he looked well. William was not well, and I was in low spirits.

Ullswater, by Joseph Wright

Group Playing Music, Sewing and Writing, by John Harden

April 21st, Wednesday. William and I sauntered a little in the garden. Coleridge came to us, and repeated the verses he wrote to Sara. I was affected with them, and was on the whole, not being well, in miserable spirits. The sunshine, the green fields, and the fair sky made me sadder; even the little happy, sporting lambs seemed but sorrowful to me. The pile wort spread out on the grass a thousand shining stars. The primroses were there, and the remains of a few daffodils. The well, which we cleaned out last night, is still but a little muddy pond, though full of water. I went to bed after dinner, could not sleep, went to bed again. Read Ferguson's life and a poem or two — fell asleep for 5 minutes and awoke better. We got tea, sate comfortably in the evening. I went to bed early.

April 22nd, Thursday. A fine mild morning — we walked into Easedale. The sun shone. Coleridge talked of his plan of sowing the laburnum in the woods. The waters were high, for there had been a great quantity of rain in the night. I was tired and sate under the shade of a holly tree that grows upon a rock, I sate there and looked down the stream. I then went to the single holly behind that single rock in the field, and sate upon the grass till they came from the waterfall. I saw them there, and heard Wm. flinging stones into the river, whose roaring was loud even where I was. When they returned, William was repeating the poem: "I have thoughts that are fed by the sun". It had been called to his mind by the dying away of the stunning of the waterfall when he came behind a stone. When we had got into the vale heavy rain came on. We saw a family of little children sheltering themselves under a wall before the rain came on; they sat in a row making a canopy for each other of their clothes. The servant lass was planting potatoes near them. Coleridge changed his clothes — we were all wet. Wilkinson came in while we were at dinner. Coleridge and I after dinner drank black currants and water.

April 23rd, 1802, Friday. It being a beautiful morning we set off at 11 o'clock, intending to stay out of doors all the morning. We went towards Rydale, and before we got to Tom Dawson's we determined to go under Nab Scar. Thither we went. The sun shone and we were lazy. Coleridge pitched upon several places to sit down upon, but we could not be all of one mind respecting sun and shade, so we pushed on to the foot of the Scar. It was very grand when we looked up, very stony, here and there a budding tree. William observed that the umbrella yew tree, that breasts the wind, had lost its character as a tree, and had become something like to solid wood. Coleridge and I pushed on before. We left William sitting on the stones, feasting with silence; and C. and I sat down upon a rocky seat — a couch it might be under the bower of William's eglantine, Andrew's Broom. He was below us, and we could see him. He came to us, and repeated his poems, while we sate beside him upon the ground. He had made himself a seat in the crumbling ground. After we had lingered long, looking into the vales,— Ambleside vale, with the copses, the village under the hill, and the green fields — Rydale, with a lake all alive and glittering, yet but little stirred by breezes, and our own dear Grasmere, first making a little round lake of nature's own, with never a house, never a green field, but the copses and the bare hills enclosing it, and the river flowing out of it. Above rose the Coniston Fells, in their own shape and colour — not man's hills, but all for themselves, the sky and the clouds, and a few wild creatures. C. went to search for something new. We saw him climbing up towards a rock. He called us, and we found him in a bower — the sweetest that was ever seen. The rock on one side is very high, and all covered with ivy, which hung loosely about, and bore bunches of brown berries. On the other side it was higher than my head. We looked down upon the Ambleside vale, that seemed to wind away from us, the village *lying* under the hill. The fir-tree island was reflected beautifully. We now first saw that the trees are planted in rows. About this bower there is mountain-ash, common-ash, yew-tree, ivy, holly, hawthorn, mosses, and flowers, and a carpet of moss. Above, at the top of the rock, there is another spot — it is scarce a bower, a little parlour on[ly], not *enclosed* by walls, but shaped out for a resting-place by the rocks, and the ground rising about it. It had a sweet moss carpet. We resolved to go and plant flowers in both these places to-morrow. We wished for Mary and Sara. Dined late. After dinner Wm. and I worked in the garden. C. read letter from Sara.

[*April*] *24th, Saturday.* A very wet day. William called me out to see a waterfall behind the barberry tree. We walked in the evening to Rydale. Coleridge and I lingered behind. C. stopped up the little runner by the road-side to make a lake. We all stood to look at Glow-worm Rock — a primrose that grew there, and just looked out on the road from its own sheltered bower. The clouds moved, as William observed, in one regular body like a multitude in motion — a sky all clouds over, not one cloud. On our return it broke a little out, and we saw here and there a star. One appeared but for a moment in a lake [of] pale blue sky.

April 25th, Sunday. After breakfast we set off with Coleridge towards Keswick. Wilkinson overtook us near the Potter's, and interrupted our discourse. C. got into a gig with Mr. Beck, and drove away from us. A shower came on, but it was soon over. We spent the morning in the orchard — read the *Prothalamium* of Spenser; walked backwards and forwards. Mr. Simpson drank tea with us. I was not well before tea. Mr. S. sent us some quills by Molly Ashburner, and his brother's book. The Luffs called at the door.

[*April*] *26th, Monday.* I copied Wm.'s poems for Coleridge. Letters from Peggy and Mary H. — wrote to Peggy and Coleridge. A terrible rain and wind all day — went to bed at 12 o'clock.

[*April*] *27th, Tuesday.* A fine morning. Mrs. Luff called. I walked with her to the boat-house. William met me at the top of the hill with his fishing-rod in his hand. I turned with him, and we sate on the hill looking to Rydale. I left him, intending to join him, but he came home, and said his lines would not stand the pulling — he had had several bites. He sate in the orchard, I made bread. Miss Simpson called, I walked with her to Goan's. When I came back I found that he and John Fisher had cleaned out the well; John had sodded about the bee-stand. In the evening Wm. began to write *The Tinker*. We had a letter and verses from Coleridge.

April 28th, Wednesday. A fine sunny but coldish morning. I copied *The Prioress's Tale*. Wm. was in the orchard. I went to him; he worked away at his poem though he was ill and tired. I happened to say that when I was a child I would not have pulled a strawberry blossom. I left him, and wrote out *The Manciple's Tale*. A dinner time he came in with the poem of *Children gathering Flowers,* but it was not quite finished, and it kept him long off his dinner. It is now done. He is working at *The Tinker*. He promised me he would get his tea, and do no more, but I have got mine an hour and a quarter, and he has scarcely begun his. I am not quite well. We have let the bright sun go down without walking. Now a heavy

Dairy Maid, by John Harden

shower comes on, and I guess we shall not walk at all. I wrote a few lines to Coleridge. Then we walked backwards and forwards between our house and Olliff's. We talked about T. Hutchinson, and Bell Addison. William left me sitting on a stone. When we came in we corrected the Chaucers, but I could not finish them to-night. Went to bed.

[*April*] *29th, Thursday.* A beautiful morning — the sun shone and all was pleasant. We sent off our parcel to Coleridge by the waggon. Mr. Simpson heard the Cuckow to-day. Before we went out, after I had written down *The Tinker,* which William finished this morning, Luff called — he was very lame, limped into the kitchen. He came on a little pony. We then went to John's Grove, sate a while at first. Afterwards William lay, and I lay, in the trench under the fence — he with his eyes shut, and listening to the waterfalls and the birds. There was no one waterfall above another — it was a sound of waters in the air — the voice of the air. William heard me breathing and rustling now and then, but we both lay still, and unseen by one another; he thought that it would be as sweet thus to lie so in the grave, to hear the *peaceful* sounds of the earth, and just to know that our dear friends were near. The lake was still; there was a boat out. Silver How reflected with delicate purple and yellowish hues, as I have seen spar; lambs on the island, and running races together by the half-dozen, in the round field near us. The copses greenish, hawthorns green. Came home to dinner, then went to Mr. Simpson — we rested a long time under a wall, sheep and lambs were in the field — cottages smoking. As I lay down on the grass, I observed the glittering silver

Moss Rose (eighteenth-century embroidery)

line on the ridge of the backs of the sheep, owing to their situation respecting the sun, which made them look beautiful, but with something of strangeness, like animals of another kind, as if belonging to a more splendid world. Met old Mrs. S. at the door — Mrs. S. poorly. I got mullins and pansies. I was sick and ill and obliged to come home soon. We went to bed immediately — I slept upstairs. The air coldish, where it was felt — somewhat frosty.

April 30th, Friday. We came into the orchard directly after breakfast, and sate there. The lake was calm, the day cloudy. We saw two fishermen by the lake side. William began to write the poem of *The Celandine*. I wrote to Mary H. sitting on the fur-gown. Walked backwards and forwards with William — he repeated his poem to me, then he got to work again and could not give over. He had not finished his dinner till 5 o'clock. After dinner we took up the fur gown into the Hollins above. We found a sweet seat, and thither we will often go. We spread the gown, put on each a cloak, and there we lay. William fell asleep — he had a bad headache owing to his having been disturbed the night before, with reading C.'s letter which Fletcher had brought to the door. I did not sleep, but I lay with half-shut eyes looking at the prospect as in a vision almost, I was so resigned to it. Loughrigg Fell was the most distant hill; then came the lake, slipping in between the copses, and above the copse the round swelling field; nearer to me, a wild intermixture of rocks, trees, and slacks of grassy ground. When we turned the corner of our little shelter, we saw the church and the whole vale. It is a blessed place. The birds were about us on all sides — skobbies, robins, bull-finches. Crows now and then flew over our heads, as we were warned by the sound of the beating of the air above. We stayed till the light of day was going, and the little birds had begun to settle their singing. But there was a thrush not far off, that seemed to sing louder and clearer than the thrushes had sung when it was quite day. We came in at 8 o'clock, got tea, wrote to Coleridge, and I wrote to Mrs. Clarkson part of a letter. We went to bed at 20 minutes past 11, with prayers that William might sleep well.

May 1st, Saturday. Rose not till half-past 8, a heavenly morning. As soon as breakfast was over, we went into the garden, and sowed the scarlet beans about the house. It was a clear sky, a heavenly morning.

I sowed the flowers, William helped me. We then went and sate in the orchard till dinner time. It was very hot. William wrote *The Celandine*. We planned a shed, for the sun was too much for us. After dinner we went again to our old resting-place in the Hollins under the rock. We first lay under a holly, where we saw nothing but the holly tree, and a budding elm [?], and the sky above our heads. But that holly tree had a beauty about it more than its own, knowing as we did where we were. When the sun had got low enough, we went to the rock shade. Oh, the overwhelming beauty of the vale below, greener than green! Two ravens flew high, high in the sky, and the sun shone upon their bellies and their wings, long after there was none of his light to be seen but a little space on the top of Loughrigg Fell. We went down to tea at 8 o'clock, had lost the poem, and returned after tea. The landscape was fading: sheep and lambs quiet among the rocks. We walked towards King's, and backwards and forwards. The sky was perfectly cloudless. N.B. Is it often so? Three solitary stars in the middle of the blue vault, one or two on the points of the high hills. Wm. wrote *The Celandine,* 2nd part to-night. Heard the cuckow to-day, this first of May.

May 2nd, Sunday. Again a heavenly morning. Letter from Coleridge.

May 4th, Tuesday. William had slept pretty well and though he went to bed nervous, and jaded in the extreme, he rose refreshed. I wrote *The Leech Gatherer* for him, which he had begun the night before, and of which he wrote several stanzas in bed this morning. It was very hot; we called at Mr. Simpson's door as we passed, but did not go in. We rested several times by the way, read, and repeated *The Leech Gatherer.* We were almost melted before we were at the top of the hill. We saw Coleridge on the Wytheburn side of the water; he crossed the beck to us. Mr. Simpson was fishing there. William and I ate a luncheon, then went on towards the waterfall. It is a glorious wild solitude under that lofty purple crag. It stood upright by itself. Its own self, and its shadow below, one mass — all else was sunshine. We went on further. A bird at the top of the crags was flying round and round, and looked in thinness and transparency, shape and motion like a moth. We climbed the hill, but looked in vain for a shade, except at the foot of the great waterfall, and there we did not like to stay on account of the loose stones above our heads. We came down, and rested upon a moss-covered rock, rising out of the bed of the river. There we lay, ate our dinner, and stayed there till about 4 o'clock or later. William and C. repeated and read verses. I drank a little brandy and water, and was in Heaven. The stag's horn is very beautiful and fresh, springing upon the fells. Mountain ashes, green. We drank tea at a farm house. The woman had not a pleasant countenance, but was civil enough. She had a pretty boy, a year old, whom she suckled. We parted from Coleridge at Sara's crag, after having looked at the letters which C. carved in the morning. I kissed

Loughrigg Mountain and River Brathay, by R. R. Reinagle

them all. William deepened the T. with C.'s pen-knife. We sate afterwards on the wall, seeing the sun go down, and the reflections in the still water. C. looked well, and parted from us chearfully, hopping up upon the side stones. On the Rays we met a woman with two little girls, one in her arms, the other, about four years old, walking by her side, a pretty little thing, but half-starved. She had on a pair of slippers that had belonged to some gentleman's child, down at the heels, but it was not easy to keep them on, but, poor thing! young as she was, she walked carefully with them; alas, too young for such cares and such travels. The mother, when we accosted her, told us that her husband had left her, and gone off with another woman, and how she *"pursued"* them. Then her fury kindled, and her eyes rolled about. She changed again to tears. She was a Cockermouth woman, thirty years of age — a child at Cockermouth when I was. I was moved, and gave her a shilling — I believe 6d. more than I ought to have given. We had the crescent moon with the "auld moon in her arms". We rested often, always upon the bridges. Reached home at about ten o'clock. The Lloyds had been here in our absence. We went soon to bed. I repeated verses to William while he was in bed; he was soothed, and I left him. "This is the spot" over and over again.

May 5th, Wednesday. A very fine morning, rather cooler than yesterday. We planted ¾ of the bower. I made bread. We sate in the orchard. The thrush sang all day, as he always sings. I wrote to the Hutchinsons, and to Coleridge — packed off *Thalaba*. William had kept off work till near bed-time, when we returned from our walk. Then he began again, and went to bed very nervous. We walked in the twilight, and walked till night came on. The moon had the old moon in her arms, but not so plain to be seen as the night before. When we went to bed it was a boat without the circle. I read *The Lover's Complaint* to Wm. in bed, and left him composed.

May 6th, Thursday. A sweet morning. We have put the finishing stroke to our bower, and here we are sitting in the orchard. It is one o'clock. We are sitting upon a seat under the wall, which I found my brother building up, when I came to him with his apple. He had intended that it should have been done before I came. It is a nice, cool, shady spot. The small birds are singing, lambs bleating, cuckow calling, the thrush sings by fits, Thomas Ashburner's axe is going quietly (without passion) in the orchard, hens are cackling, flies humming, the women talking together at their doors, plumb and pear trees are in blossom — apple trees greenish — the opposite woods green, the crows are cawing. We have heard ravens. The ash trees are in blossom, birds flying all about us. The stitchwort is coming out, there is one budding lychnis, the primroses are passing their prime, celandine, violets, and wood sorrel for ever more, little geraniums and pansies on the wall. We walked in the evening to Tail End, to enquire about hurdles for the orchard shed and about Mr. Luff's flower. The flower dead! no hurdles. I went on to look at the falling wood; Wm. also, when he had been at Benson's, went with me. They have left a good many small oak trees but we dare not hope that they are all to remain. The ladies are come to Mr. Gell's cottage. We saw them as we went, and their light when we returned. When we came in we found a Magazine, and Review, and a letter from Coleridge with verses to Hartley, and Sara H. We

read the review, etc. The moon was a perfect boat, a silver boat, when we were out in the evening. The birch tree is all over green in *small* leaf, more light and elegant than when it is full out. It bent to the breezes, as if for the love of its own delightful motions. Sloe-thorns and hawthorns in the hedges.

May 7th, Friday. William had slept uncommonly well, so, feeling himself strong, he fell to work at *The Leech Gatherer*; he wrote hard at it till dinner time, then he gave over, tired to death — he had finished the poem. I was making Derwent's frocks. After dinner we sate in the orchard. It was a thick, hazy, dull air. The thrush sang almost continually; the little birds were more than usually busy with their voices. The sparrows are now full fledged. The nest is so full that they lie upon one another, they sit quietly in their nest with closed mouths. I walked to Rydale after tea, which we drank by the kitchen fire. The evening very dull — a terrible kind of threatening brightness at sunset above Easedale. The sloe-thorn beautiful in the hedges, and in the wild spots higher up among the hawthorns. No letters. William met me. He had been digging in my absence, and cleaning the well. We walked up beyond Lewthwaites. A very dull sky; coolish; crescent moon now and then. I had a letter brought me from Mrs. Clarkson while we were walking in the orchard. I observed the sorrel leaves opening at about 9 o'clock. William went to bed tired with thinking about a poem.

May 8th, Saturday Morning. We sowed the scarlet beans in the orchard, and read *Henry V.* there. William lay on his back on the seat. I wept "For names, sounds, faiths, delights and duties lost" — taken from a poem upon Cowley's wish to retire to the Plantations. Read in the Review. I finished Derwent's frocks. After dinner William added a step to the orchard steps.

May 9th, Sunday Morning. The air considerably colder to-day, but the sun shone

Major Gilpin Shearing a Sheep, by John Harden

all day. William worked at *The Leech Gatherer* almost incessantly from morning till tea-time. I copied *The Leech Gatherer* and other poems for Coleridge. I was oppressed and sick at heart, for he wearied himself to death. After tea he wrote two stanzas in the manner of Thomson's *Castle of Indolence,* and was tired out. Bad news of Coleridge.

May 10th, Monday. A fine clear morning, but coldish. William is still at work, though it is past ten o'clock—he will be tired out, I am sure. My heart fails in me. He worked a little at odd things, but after dinner he gave over. An affecting letter from Mary H. We sate in the orchard before dinner. Old Joyce spent the day. I wrote to Mary H. Mrs. Jameson and Miss Simpson called just when William was going to bed at 8 o'clock. I wrote to Coleridge, sent off reviews and poems. Went to bed at 12 o'clock. William did not sleep till 3 o'clock.

May 11th, Tuesday. A cool air. William finished the stanzas about C. and himself. He did not go out to-day. Miss Simpson came in to tea, which was lucky enough, for it interrupted his labours. I walked with her to Rydale. The evening cool; the moon only now and then to be seen; the Lake purple as we went; primroses still in abundance. William did not meet me. He completely finished his poems, I finished Derwent's frocks. We went to bed at 12 o'clock. Wm. pretty well — he looked very well — he complains that he gets cold in his chest.

May 12th, Wednesday. A sunshiny, but coldish morning. We walked into

Easedale and returned by George Rawnson's and the lane. We brought home heckberry blossom, crab blossom, the anemone nemorosa, marsh marigold, speedwell — that beautiful blue one, the colour of the blue-stone or glass used in jewellery — with its beautiful pearl-like chives. Anemones are in abundance, and still the dear dear primroses, violets in beds, pansies in abundance, and the little celandine. I pulled a bunch of the taller celandine. Butterflies of all colours. I often see some small ones of a pale purple lilac, or emperor's eye colour, something of the colour of that large geranium which grows by the lake side. Wm. observed the beauty of Geordy Green's[1] house. We see it from our Orchard.

1. *i.e.* Pavement End.

Wm. pulled ivy with beautiful berries — I put it over the chimneypiece. Sate in the orchard the hour before dinner, coldish. We have now dined. My head aches — William is sleeping in the window. In the evening we were sitting at the table, writing, when we were rouzed by Coleridge's voice below. He had walked; looked palish, but was not much tired. We sate up till one o'clock, all together; then William went to bed, and I sate with C. in the sitting-room (where he slept) till a ¼ past 2 o'clock. Wrote to M. H.

May 13th, Thursday. The day was very cold, with snow showers. Coleridge had intended going in the morning to Keswick, but the cold and showers

hindered him. We went with him after tea as far as the plantations by the roadside descending to Wytheburn. He did not look very well when we parted from him. We sate an hour at Mrs. Simpson's.

May 14th, Friday. A very cold morning — hail and snow showers all day. We went to Brother's wood, intending to get plants, and to go along the shore of the lake to the foot. We did go a part of the way, but there was no pleasure in stepping along that difficult sauntering road in this ungenial weather. We turned again, and walked backwards and forwards in Brother's wood. William teased himself with seeking an epithet for the cuckow. I sate a while upon my last summer seat, the mossy stone. William's, unemployed, beside me, and the space between, where Coleridge has so often lain. The oak trees are just putting forth yellow knots of leaves. The ashes with their flowers passing away, and leaves coming out. The blue hyacinth is not quite full blown; gowans are coming out, marsh marigolds in full glory; the little star plant, a star without a flower. We took home a great load of gowans, and planted them in the cold about the orchard. After dinner, I worked bread, then came and mended stockings beside William; he fell asleep. After tea I walked to Rydale for letters. It was a strange night. The hills were covered over with a slight covering of hail or snow, just so as to give them a hoary winter look with the black rocks. The woods looked miserable, the coppices green as grass, which looked quite unnatural, and they seemed half shrivelled up, as if they shrank from the air. O, thought I! what a beautiful thing God has made winter to be, by stripping the trees, and letting us

SKYLARK.

see their shapes and forms. What a freedom does it seem to give to the storms! There were several new flowers out, but I had no pleasure in looking at them. I walked as fast as I could back again with my letter from S. H. which I skimmed over at Tommy Fleming's. Met Wm. at the top of White Moss. We walked a little beyond Olliff's. Near 10 when we came in. Wm. and Molly had dug the ground and planted potatoes in my absence. We wrote to Coleridge; sent off a letter to Annette, bread and frocks to the C.'s. Went to bed at ½-past 11. William very nervous. After he was in bed, haunted with altering *The Rainbow*.

May 15th, Saturday Morning. It is now ¼ past 10, and he is not up. Miss Simpson called when I was in bed. I have been in the garden. It looks fresh and neat in spite of the frost. Molly tells me they had thick ice on a jug at their door last night. A very cold and chearless morning. I sate mending stockings all the morning. I read in Shakespeare. William lay very late because he slept ill last night. It snowed this morning just like Christmas. We had a melancholy letter from Coleridge just at bed-time. It distressed me very much, and I resolved upon going to Keswick the next day.

[*The following is written on the blotting-paper opposite this date:*]

S. T. Coleridge.

Dorothy Wordsworth. William Wordsworth.

Mary Hutchinson. Sara Hutchinson.

William. Coleridge. Mary.

Dorothy. Sara.

16th May.

1802.

John Wordsworth.

[*May*] 16*th, Sunday*. William was at work all the morning. I did not go to Keswick. A sunny, cold, frosty day. A snow-shower at night. We were a good while in the orchard in the morning.

May 17th, Monday. William was not well, he went with me to Wytheburn water. He left me in a post-chaise. Hail showers, snow, and cold attacked me. The people were graving peats under Nadel Fell. A lark and thrush singing near Coleridge's house. Bancrofts there. A letter from M. H.

May 18th, Tuesday. Terribly cold, Coleridge not well. Froude called, Wilkinsons called, I not well. C. and I walked in the evening in the garden. Warmer in the evening. Wrote to M. and S.

May 19th, Wednesday. A grey morning — not quite so cold. C. and I set off at ½-past 9 o'clock. Met William near the 6-mile stone. We sate down by the road-side, and then went to Wytheburn water. Longed to be at the island. Sate in the sun. Coleridge's bowels bad, mine also. We drank tea at John Stanley's. The evening cold and clear. A glorious light on Skiddaw. I was tired. Brought a cloak down from Mr. Simpson's. Packed up books for Coleridge, then got supper, and went to bed.

May 20th, Thursday. A frosty, clear morning. I lay in bed late. William got to work. I was somewhat tired. We sate in the orchard sheltered all the morning. In the evening there was a fine rain. We received a letter from Coleridge, telling us that he wished us not to go to Keswick.

, *May 21st, Friday.* A very warm gentle morning, a little rain. William wrote two sonnets on Buonaparte, after I had read Milton's sonnets to him. In the evening he went with Mr. Simpson with Borwick's boat to gather ling in Bainriggs. I planted about the well, was much heated, and I think I caught cold.

May 22nd, Saturday. A very hot morning. A hot wind, as if coming from a sand desert. We met Coleridge. He was sitting under Sara's rock when we reached him. He turned with us. We sate a long time under the wall of a sheep-fold. Had some interesting melancholy talk about his private affairs. We drank tea at a farmhouse. The woman was very kind. There was a woman with 3 children travelling from Workington to Manchester. The woman served them liberally. Afterwards she said that she never suffered any to go away without a trifle "sec as we have". The woman at whose house we drank tea the last time was rich and senseless — she said "she never served any but their own poor". C. came home with us. We sate some time in the orchard. Then they came into supper — mutton chops and potatoes. Letters from S. and M. H.

[*May 23rd,*] *Sunday.* I sate with C. in the orchard all the morning. I was ill in the afternoon, took laudanum. We walked in Bainriggs after tea. Saw the juniper — umbrella shaped. C. went to S. and M. Points,[1] joined us on White Moss.

1. Mary Point and Sara Point; the "two heath-clad rocks" referred to in the last of the *Poems on the Naming of Places.*

May 24th, Monday. A very hot morning. We were ready to go off with Coleridge, but foolishly sauntered, and Miss Taylor and Miss Stanley called. William and Coleridge and I went afterwards to the top of the Rays.

I had sent off a letter to Mary by C. I wrote again, and to C. Then went to bed. William slept not till 5 o'clock.

[*May*] 25*th, Tuesday.* Very hot — I went to bed after dinner. We walked in the

Derwentwater with Skiddaw, by Joseph Wright

evening. Papers and short note from C.; again no sleep for Wm.

[*May*] 26*th, Wednesday*. I was very unwell — went to bed again after dinner. We walked a long time backwards and forwards between John's Grove and the lane upon the turf. A beautiful night, not cloudless. It has never been so since May day.

[*May*] 27*th, Thursday*. I was in bed all day — very ill. William wrote to Rd., Cr. and Cook. Wm. went after tea into the orchard. I slept in his bed — he slept downstairs.

[*May*] 28*th, Friday*. I was much better than yesterday, though poorly. William tired himself with hammering at a passage. After dinner he was better and I greatly better. We sate in the orchard. The sky cloudy, the air sweet and cool. The young bullfinches, in their party-coloured raiment, bustle about among the blossoms, and poize themselves like wire-dancers or tumblers, shaking the twigs and dashing off the blossoms. There is yet one primrose in the orchard. The stitchwort is fading. The wild columbines are coming into beauty, the vetches are in abundance, blossoming and seeding. That pretty little wavy-looking dial-like yellow flower, the speedwell, and some others, whose names I do not yet know. The wild columbines are coming into beauty—some of the gowans fading. In the garden we have lilies, and many other flowers. The scarlet beans are up in crowds. It is now between 8 and nine o'clock. It has rained sweetly for two hours

I GRIEVED FOR BUONAPARTÉ
(Published as 1801)

I grieved for Buonaparté, with a vain
And an unthinking grief! The tenderest mood
Of that Man's mind — what can it be? what food
Fed his first hopes? what knowledge could *he* gain?
'Tis not in battles that from youth we train
The Governor who must be wise and good,
And temper with the sternness of the brain
Thoughts motherly, and meek as womanhood.
Wisdom doth live with children round her knees:
Books, leisure, perfect freedom, and the talk
Man holds with week-day man in the hourly walk
Of the mind's business: these are the degrees
By which true Sway doth mount; this is the stalk
True Power doth grow on; and her rights are these.

William Wordsworth

and a half; the air is very mild. The heckberry blossoms are dropping off fast, almost gone — barberries are in beauty — snowballs coming forward — May roses blossoming.

[*May*] 29*th, Saturday*. I was much better — I made bread and a wee rhubarb tart and batter pudding for William. We sate in the orchard after dinner. William finished his poem on going for Mary. I wrote it out. I wrote to Mary H., having received a letter from her in the evening. A sweet day. We nailed up the honeysuckles, and hoed the scarlet beans.

May 30*th, Sunday*. I wrote to Mrs. Clarkson. It was a clear but cold day. The Simpsons called in the evening. I had been obliged to go to bed before tea, and was unwell all day. Gooseberries, a present from Peggy Hodgson. I wrote to my Aunt Cookson.

[*May*] 31*st, Monday*. I was much better. We sat out all day. Mary Jameson dined. I wrote out the poem on "Our Departure", which he seemed to have finished. In the evening Miss Simpson brought us a letter from M. H., and a complimentary and critical letter to W. from John Wilson of Glasgow, post-paid. I went a little way with Miss S. My tooth broke today. They will soon be gone. Let that pass, I shall be beloved — I want no more.

[*June* 1*st,*] *Tuesday*. A very sweet day, but a sad want of rain. We went into the orchard before dinner, after I had written to M. H. Then on to Mr. Olliff's intakes. We found some torn birds nests. The columbine was growing upon the rocks; here and there a solitary plant, sheltered and shaded by the tufts and bowers

of trees. It is a graceful slender creature, a female seeking retirement, and growing freest and most graceful where it is most alone. I observed that the more shaded plants were always the tallest. A short note and gooseberries from Coleridge.

June 2nd, Wednesday. In the morning we observed that the scarlet beans were drooping in the leaves in great numbers, owing, we guess, to an insect. We sate awhile in the orchard — then we went to the old carpenter's about the hurdles. Yesterday an old man called, a grey-headed man, above 70 years of age. He said he had been a soldier, that his wife and children had died in Jamaica. He had a beggar's wallet over his shoulders; a coat of shreds and patches, altogether of a drab colour; he was tall, and though his body was bent, he had the look of one used to have been upright. I talked a while, and then gave him a piece of cold bacon and a penny. Said he, "You're a fine woman!" I could not help smiling; I suppose he meant, "You're a kind woman". Afterwards a woman called, travelling to Glasgow. After dinner we went into Frank's field, crawled up the little glen, and planned a seat, then went to Mr. Olliff's Hollins and sate there — found a beautiful shell-like purple fungus in Frank's field. After tea we walked to Butterlip How, and backwards and forwards there. All the young oak tree leaves are dry as powder. A cold south wind, portending rain. I ought to have said that on Tuesday evening, namely June 1st, we walked upon the turf near John's Grove. It was a lovely night. The clouds of the western sky reflected a saffron light upon the upper end of the lake. All was still. We went to look at Rydale. There was an Alpine, fire-like red upon the tops of the mountains. This was gone when we came in view of the lake. But we saw the Lake in a new and most beautiful point of view, between two little rocks, and behind a small ridge that had concealed it from us. This White Moss, a place made for all kinds of beautiful works of art and nature, woods and valleys, fairy valleys and fairy tarns, miniature mountains, alps above alps. Little John Dawson came in from the woods with a stick over his shoulder.

June 3rd, 1802, Thursday. A very fine rain. I lay in bed till ten o'clock. William much better than yesterday. We walked into Easedale — sheltered in a cow-house — came home wet. The cuckow sang, and we watched the little birds as we sate at the door of the cow-house. The oak copses are brown, as in autumn, with the late frosts — scattered over with green trees, birches or hazels. The ashes are coming into full leaf, some of them injured. We came home quite wet. We have been reading the life and some of the writings of poor Logan since dinner. "And everlasting longings for the lost." It is an affecting line. There are many affecting lines and passages in his poem. William is now sleeping, with the window open, lying on the window seat. The thrush is singing. There are, I do believe, a thousand buds on the honeysuckle tree, all small and far from blowing, save one that is retired behind the twigs close to the wall, and as snug as a bird's nest. John's rose tree is very beautiful, blended with the honeysuckle.

On Tuesday evening when we were among the rocks we saw in the woods what seemed to be a man resting or looking about him — he had a piece of wood near him. William was on before me when we returned and as I was going up to

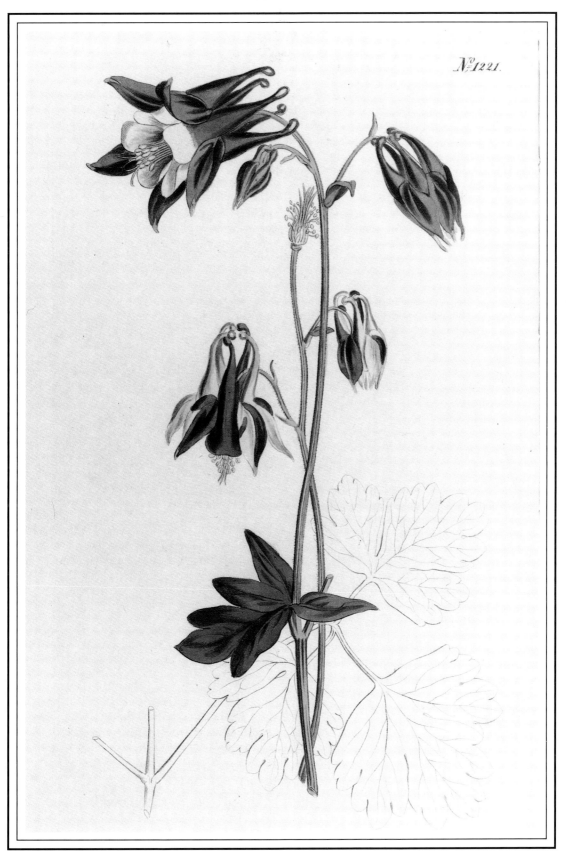

'. . . columbines are coming into beauty.'

him I found that this supposed man was John Dawson. I spoke to him and I suppose he thought I asked him what my Brother had said to him before, for he replied: "*William* asks me how my head is". Poor fellow — he says it is worse and worse, and he walks as if he were afraid of putting his body in motion.

Yesterday morning William walked as far as the Swan with Aggy Fisher. She was going to attend upon Goan's dying infant. She said, "There are many heavier crosses than the death of an infant"; and went on, "There was a woman in this vale who buried 4 grown-up children in one year, and I have heard her say, when many years were gone by, that she had more pleasure in thinking of those 4 than of her living children, for as children get up and have families of their own, their duty to their parents *'wears out and weakens'*. She could trip lightly by the graves of those who died when they were young with a light step, as she went to church on a Sunday."

We walked while dinner was getting ready up into Mr. King's Hollins. I was weak and made my way down alone, for Wm. took a difficult way. After dinner we walked upon the turf path — a showery afternoon. A very affecting letter came from M. H., while I was sitting in the window reading Milton's *Penseroso* to William. I answered this letter before I went to bed.

June 4th, Friday. It was a very sweet morning. There had been much rain in the night. Dined late. In the evening we walked on our favourite path. Then we came in and sate in the orchard. The evening was dark and warm — a tranquil night. I left William in the orchard. I read *Mother Hubbard's Tale* before I went to bed.

[June] 5th, Saturday. A fine showery morning. I made both pies and bread; but we first walked into Easedale, and sate under the oak trees, upon the mossy stones. There were one or two slight showers. The gowans were flourishing along the banks of the stream. The strawberry flower (Geum) hanging over the brook — all things soft and green. In the afternoon William sate in the orchard. I went there, was tired, and fell asleep. Mr. Simpson drank tea, Mrs. Smith called with her daughter. We began the letter to John Wilson.

June 6th, Sunday. A showery morning. We were writing the letter to John Wilson when Ellen came. Molly at Goan's child's funeral. After dinner I walked into John Fisher's intake with Ellen. She brought us letters from Coleridge, Mrs. Clarkson, and Sara Hutchinson. William went out in the evening and sate in the orchard, it was a showery day. In the evening there was one of the heaviest showers I ever remember.

June 7th, Monday. I wrote to Mary H. this morning, sent the C. Indolence poem. Copied the letter to John Wilson, and wrote to my brother Richard and Mrs. Coleridge. In the evening I walked with Ellen to Butterlip How and to George Mackareth's for the horse. It was a very sweet evening; there was the cuckow and the little birds; the copses still injured, but the trees in general looked most soft and beautiful in tufts. William was walking when we came in — he had slept miserably for 2 nights past, so we all went to bed soon. I went with Ellen in the morning to Rydale Falls. Letters from Annette, Mary H. and Cook.

June 8th, Tuesday. Ellen and I rode to Windermere. We had a fine sunny day, neither hot nor cold. I mounted the horse at the quarry. We had no difficulties or delays but at the gates. I was enchanted with some of the views. From the High Ray the view is very delightful, rich, and festive, water and wood, houses, groves, hedgerows, green fields, and mountains; white houses, large and small. We passed 2 or 3 nice-looking statesmen's houses. Mr. Curwen's shrubberies looked pitiful enough under the native trees. We put up our horses, ate our dinner by the water-side, and walked up to the Station. Then we went to the Island, walked round it, and crossed the lake with our horse in the ferry. The shrubs have been cut away in some parts of the island. I observed to the boatman that I did not think it improved. He replied: "We think it is, for one could hardly see the house before". It seems to me to be, however, no better than it was. They have made no natural glades; it is merely a lawn with a few miserable young trees, standing as if they were half-starved. There are no sheep, no cattle upon these lawns. It is neither one thing or another — neither *natural,* nor wholly cultivated and artificial, which it was before. And that great house! Mercy upon us! if it *could* be concealed, it *would* be well for all who are not pained to see the pleasantest of earthly spots deformed by man. But it *cannot* be covered. Even the tallest of our old oak trees would not reach to the top of it. When we went into the boat, there were two men standing at the landing-place. One seemed to be about 60, a man with a jolly red face; he looked as if he might have lived many years in Mr.

Curwen's house. He wore a blue jacket and trowsers, as the people who live close by Windermere, particularly at the places of chief resort, in affectation, I suppose. He looked significantly at our boatman just as we were rowing off, and said, "Thomas, mind you take off the directions off that cask. You know what I mean. It will serve as a blind for them, *you* know. It was a blind business, both for you, and the coachman, and me and all of us. Mind you take off the directions. A wink's as good as a nod with some folks"; and then he turned round, looking at his companion with such an air of self-satisfaction, and deep insight into unknown things! I could hardly help laughing outright at him. Laburnums blossom freely at the island, and in the shrubberies on the shore — they are blighted everywhere else. Roses of various sorts now out. The brooms were in full glory everywhere, "veins of gold" among the copses. The hawthorns in the valley fading away — beautiful upon the hills. We reached home at 3 o'clock. After tea William went out and walked and wrote that poem, "The sun has long been set", etc. He first went up to G. Mackareth's with the horse, afterwards he walked on our own path and wrote the lines; he called me into the orchard, and there repeated them to me — he then stayed there till 11 o'clock.

CRATÆGUS *Hawthorn.*

A View on Lake Windermere, by J. C. Ibbetson

June 9th, Wednesday. Wm. slept ill. A soaking all day rain. We should have gone to Mr. Simpson's to tea but we walked up after tea. Lloyds called. The hawthorns on the mountain sides like orchards in blossom. Brought rhubarb down. It rained hard. Ambleside fair. I wrote to Christr. and M. H.

June 10th, Thursday. I wrote to Mrs. Clarkson and Luff — went with Ellen to Rydale. Coleridge came in with a sack full of books, etc., and a branch of mountain ash. He had been attacked by a cow. He came over by Grisdale. A furious wind. Mr. Simpson drank tea. William very poorly — we went to bed latish — I slept in sitting room.

June 11th, Friday. A wet day. William had slept very ill. Wm. and C. walked out. I went to bed after dinner, not well. I was tired with making beds, cooking etc., Molly being very ill.

June 12th, Saturday. A rainy morning. C. set off before dinner. We went with him to the Rays, but it rained, so we went no further. Sheltered under a wall. He would be sadly wet, for a furious shower came on just when we parted. We got no dinner, but gooseberry pie to our tea. I baked both pies and bread, and walked with William, first on our own path, but it was too wet there, next over the rocks to the road, and backward and forward, and last of all up to Mr. King's. Miss Simpson and Robert had called. Letters from Sara and Annette.

June 13th, Sunday. A fine morning. Sunshiny and bright, but with rainy clouds. William had slept better but not well, he has been altering the poem to Mary this morning, he is now washing his feet. I wrote out poems for our journey and I wrote a letter to my Uncle Cookson. Mr. Simpson came when we were in the orchard in the morning, and brought us a beautiful drawing which he had done. In the evening we walked, first on our own path — there we walked a good while. It was a silent night. The stars were out by ones and twos, but no cuckow, no little birds, the air was not warm, and we have observed that since Tuesday, 8th, when William wrote, "The sun has long been set", that we have had no birds singing after the evening is fairly set in. We walked to our new view of Rydale, but it put on a sullen face. There was an owl hooting in Bainriggs. Its first halloo

was so like a human shout that I was surprized, when it made its second call tremulous and lengthened out, to find that the shout had come from an owl. The full moon (not quite full) was among a company of steady island clouds, and the sky bluer about it than the natural sky blue. William observed that the full moon, above a dark fir grove, is a fine image of the descent of a superior being. There was a shower which drove us into John's Grove before we had quitted our favourite path. We walked upon John's path before we went to view Rydale. We went to bed immediately upon our return home.

June 14th, Monday. I was very unwell — went to bed before I drank my tea — was sick and afterwards almost asleep when William brought me a letter from Mary, which he read to me sitting by the bed-side. Wm. wrote to Mary and Sara about *The Leech Gatherer,* I wrote to both of them in one and to Annette, to Coleridge also. I was better after tea — I walked with Wm. when I had put up my parcel, on our own path. We were driven away by the horses that go on the commons; then we went to look at Rydale, walked a little in the fir grove, went again to the top of the hill, and came home. A mild and sweet night. William stayed behind me. I threw him the cloak out of the window. The moon overcast. He sate a few minutes in the orchard, came in sleepy, and hurried to bed. I carried him his bread and butter.

[*June*] *15th, Tuesday.* A sweet, grey, mild morning. The birds sing soft and low. William has not slept all night. It wants only 10 minutes of 10, and he is in bed yet. After William rose we went and sate in the orchard till dinner time. We

walked a long time in the evening upon our favourite path; the owls hooted, the night hawk sang to itself incessantly, but there were no little birds, no thrushes. I left William writing a few lines about the night-hawk and other images of the evening, and went to seek for letters. None were come. We walked backwards and forwards a little, after I returned to William, and then up as far as Mr. King's. Came in. There was a basket of lettuces, a letter from M. H. about the delay of mine, and telling of one she had sent by the other post, one from Wade, and one from Sara to C. William did not read them. M. H. growing fat.

June 16th, Wednesday. We walked towards Rydale for letters — met Frank Batey with the expected one from Mary. We went up into Rydale woods and read it there. We sate near an old wall, which fenced a hazel grove, which Wm. said was exactly like the filbert grove at Middleham. It is a beautiful spot, a sloping or rather steep piece of ground, with hazels growing "tall and erect" in clumps at distances, almost seeming regular, as if they had been planted. We returned to dinner. I wrote to Mary after dinner, while William sate in the orchard. Old Mr. Simpson drank tea with us. When Mr. S. was gone I read my letter to William, speaking to Mary about having a cat. I spoke of the little birds keeping us company, and William told me that that very morning a bird had perched upon his leg. He had been lying very still, and had watched this little creature, it had come under the bench where he was sitting, and then flew up to his leg; he thoughtlessly stirred himself to look further at it, and it flew on to the apple tree above him. It was a little young creature, that had just left its nest, equally unacquainted with man, and unaccustomed to struggle against storms and winds. While it was upon the apple tree the wind blew about the stiff boughs, and the bird seemed bemazed, and not strong enough to strive with it. The swallows come to the sitting-room window as if wishing to build, but I am afraid they will not have courage for it, but I believe they will build in my room window. They twitter, and make a bustle and a little chearful song, hanging against the panes of glass, with their soft white bellies close to the glass, and their forked fish-like tails. They swim round and round, and again they come. It was a sweet evening. We first walked to the top of the hill to look at Rydale, then to Butterlip How. I do not now see the brownness that was in the coppices. The lower hawthorn blossoms passed away. Those on the hills are a faint white. The wild guelder-rose is coming out, and the wild roses. I have seen no honey-suckles yet, except our own one nestling, and a tree of the yellow kind at Mrs. Townley's the day I went with Ellen to Windermere. Foxgloves are now frequent, the first I saw was that day with Ellen and the first ripe strawberries. William went to bed immediately.

[June] 17th, Thursday. William had slept well. I took castor oil and lay in bed till 12 o'clock. William injured himself with working a little. When I got up we sate in the orchard — a sweet mild day. Miss Hudson called — I went with her to the top of the hill. When I came home I found William at work attempting to alter a stanza in the poem on our going for Mary, which I convinced him did not need altering. We sate in the house after dinner. In the evening walked on our favourite path. A short letter from Coleridge. Willliam added a little to the Ode he is

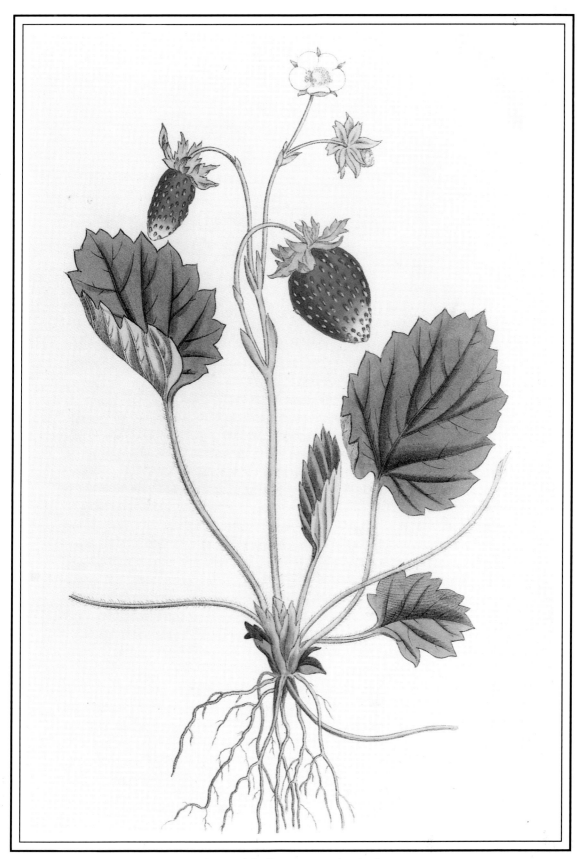

'. . . and the first ripe strawberries.'

SWALLOW.

June 18th, Friday. When we were sitting after breakfast — William about to shave — Luff came in. It was a sweet morning — he had rode over the Fells. He brought news about Lord Lowther's intention to pay all debts, etc., and a letter from Mr. Clarkson. He saw our garden, was astonished at the scarlet beans, etc. etc. When he was gone, we wrote to Coleridge, M. H., and my brother Richard about the affair. William determined to go to Eusemere on Monday. In the afternoon we walked to Rydale with our letters — found no letters there. A sweet evening. I had a woful headache, and was ill in stomach from agitation of mind — went ot bed at nine o'clock, but did not sleep till late.

[*June*] 19*th, Saturday*. The swallows were very busy under my window this morning. I slept pretty well, but William has got no sleep. It is after 11 and he is still in bed. A fine morning. Coleridge, when he was last here, told us that for many years, there being no Quaker meeting held at Keswick, a single old Quaker woman used to go regularly alone every Sunday to attend the meeting-house, and there used to sit and perform her worship, alone in that beautiful place among those fir trees, in that spacious vale, under the great mountain Skiddaw!!! Poor old Willy — we never pass by his grave close to the Churchyard gate without thinking of him and having his figure brought back to our minds. He formerly was an ostler at Hawkshead having spent a little estate. In his old age he was boarded or as they say *let* by the parish. A boy of the house that hired him was riding one morning pretty briskly beside John Fisher's — "Hullo! has aught particular happened?" said John to the boy — "Nay, naught at aw, nobbut auld Willy's dead." He was going to order the passing bell to be tolled. On Thursday morning Miss Hudson of Workington called. She said, "O! I love flowers! I sow flowers in the parks several miles from home, and my mother and I visit them, and watch them how they grow." This may show that botanists may be often deceived when they find rare flowers growing far from houses. This was a very ordinary young woman, such as in any town in the North of England one may find a score. I sate up a while after William — he then called me down to him. (I was writing to Mary H.) I read Churchill's *Rosciad.* Returned again to my writing, and did not go to bed till he called to me. The shutters were closed, but I heard the birds singing. There was our own thrush, shouting with an impatient shout — so it sounded to me. The morning was still, the twittering of the little birds was very gloomy. The owls had hooted a ¼ of an hour before, now the cocks were crowing. It was near daylight, I put out my candle, and went to bed. In a little time I thought I heard William snoring, so I composed myself to sleep. Charles Lloyd called. [?] at my sweet Brother.

June 20th, Sunday. He had slept better than I could have expected, but he was far from well all day; we were in the orchard a great part of the morning. After tea we walked upon our own path for a long time. We talked sweetly together about the disposal of our riches. We lay upon the sloping turf. Earth and sky were so lovely that they melted our very hearts. The sky to the north was of a chastened yet rich yellow, fading into pale blue, and streaked and scattered over with steady islands of purple, melting away into shades of pink. It made my heart almost feel like a vision to me. We afterwards took our cloaks and sate in the orchard. Mr. and Miss Simpson called. We told them of our expected good fortune. We were astonished and somewhat hurt to see how coldly Mr. Simpson received it — Miss S. seemed very glad. We went into the house when they left us, and Wm. went to bed. I sate up about an hour. He then called me to talk to him — he could not fall asleep. I wrote to Montagu.

[*June*] *21st, Monday*. William was obliged to be in bed late, he had slept so miserably. It was a very fine morning, but as we did not leave home till 12 o'clock it was very hot. I parted from my Beloved in the green lane above the Black- smith's, then went to dinner at Mr. Simpson's — we walked afterwards in the garden. Betty Towers and her son and daughter came to tea. The little lad is 4 years old, almost as little a thing as Hartley, and as sharp too, they say, but I saw nothing of this, being a stranger, except in his bonny eyes, which had such a sweet brightness in them when any thing was said to him that made him ashamed and draw his chin into his neck, while he sent his eyes upwards to look at you. His Mother is a delicate woman. She said she thought that both she and her husband were so tender in their health that they must be obliged to sell their land. Speaking

Exterior Group, Ambleside,
by John Harden

of old Jim Jackson she said: "They might have looked up with the best in Grasmere, if they had but been careful" — "They began with a clear estate, and had never had but one child, he to be sure is a half-wit" — "How did they get through with their money?" — "Why in eating and drinking. The wife would make tea 4 or 5 times in a day and sec' folks for sugar! Then she would have nea Teapot, but she would take the water out of a brass pan on the fire and pour it on the tea in a quart pot. This all for herself, for she boiled the tea leaves always for her husband and their son."

I brought plants home, sunflowers, and planted them.

Aggy Fisher was talking with me on Monday morning, 21st of June, about her son. She went on — Old Mary Watson was at Goan's there when the child died. I had never seen her before since her son was drowned last summer, "we were all in trouble and trouble opens folks' hearts". She began to tell about her daughter that's married to Leonard Holmes, how now that sickness is come upon him they are breaking down and failing in the world. Debts are coming in every day, and he can do nothing, and they fret and jar together. One day he came riding over to Grasmere — I wondered what was the matter, and I resolved to speak to him when he came back. He was as pale as a ghost, and he did not suffer the horse to gang quicker than a snail could crawl. He had come over in a trick of passion to auld Mary to tell her she might take her own again, her daughter and the bairns. Mary replied nobly (said Aggy) that she would not part man and wife, but that all should come together, and she would keep them while she had anything. Old Mary went to see them at Ambleside afterwards, and he begged her pardon. Aggy observed that they would never have known this sorrow, if it had pleased God to take him off suddenly.

[*June 22nd,*] *Tuesday Morning.* I had my breakfast in bed, being not quite well — I then walked to Rydale, I waited long for the post, lying in the field, and looking at the distant mountains, — looking and listening to the river. I met the post.

Letters from Montagu and Richard. I hurried back, forwarded these to William, and wrote to Montagu. When I came home I wrote to my brother Christopher. I could settle to nothing. Molly washed and glazed the curtains. I read the *Midsummer Night's Dream,* and began *As You Like It.* Miss Simpson called — Tamar brought me some berries. I resolved to go to William and for that purpose John Fisher promised to go over the fells with me. Miss Simpson ate pie, and then left me reading letters from Mary and Coleridge. The news came that a house was taken for Betsy. I wrote to Mary H. and put up a parcel for Coleridge. The L.B. arrived. I went to bed at ½ past 11.

June 23rd, Wednesday. I slept till ½ past 3 o'clock — called Molly before 4, and had got myself dressed and breakfasted before 5, but it rained and I went to bed again. It is now 20 minutes past 10 — a sunshiny morning. I walked to the top of the hill and sate under a wall near John's Grove, facing the sun. I read a scene or two in *As You Like It.* I met Charles Lloyd, and old Mr. Lloyd was upstairs — Mrs. Ll. had been to meet me. I wrote a line to Wm. by the Lloyds. Coleridge and Leslie came just as I had lain down after dinner. C. brought me W.'s letter. He had got well to Eusemere. C. and I accompanied Leslie to the boat-house. It was a sullen, coldish evening, no sunshine; but after we had parted from Leslie a light came out suddenly that repaid us for all. It fell only upon one hill, and the island, but it arrayed the grass and trees in gem-like brightness. I cooked C. his supper. We sate up till one o'clock.

June 24th, Thursday. I went with C. half-way up the Rays. It was a cool morning. I dined at Mr. Simpson's and helped Aggy Fleming to quilt a petticoat. Miss Simpson came with me after tea round by the White Bridge. I ground paint when I reached home, and was tired. Wm. came in just when Molly had left me. It was a mild rainy evening — he was cool and fresh and smelt sweetly — his clothes were wet. We sate together talking till the first dawning of day — a happy time. He was pale and not much tired. He thought I looked well too.

June 25th, Friday. Wm. had not fallen asleep till after 3 o'clock, but he slept tolerably. Miss Simpson came to colour the rooms. I began with whitewashing the ceiling. I worked with them (William was very busy) till dinner time, but after dinner I went to bed and fell asleep. When I rose I went just before tea in the garden. I looked up at my swallow's nest, and it was gone. It had fallen down. Poor little creatures, they could not themselves be more distressed than I was. I went upstairs to look at the ruins. They lay in a large heap upon the window ledge; these swallows had been ten days employed in building this nest, and it seemed to be almost finished. I had watched them early in the morning, in the day many and many a time, and in the evenings when it was almost dark. I had seen them sitting together side by side in their unfinished nest, both morning and night. When they first came about the window they used to hang against the panes, with their white bellies and their forked tails, looking like fish; but then they fluttered and sang their own little twittering song. As soon as the nest was broad enough, a sort of ledge for them, they sate both mornings and evenings, but they did not pass the night there. I watched them one morning, when William was at Eusemere, for more than an hour. Every now and then there was a feeling motion in their wings, a sort of tremulousness, and they sang a low song to one another.

[*June 29th Tuesday. . . .*][1] that they would not call here, I was going to tea. It is an uncertain day, sunshine, showers, and wind. It is now 8

1. A page torn out of the MS. here. Among other things it must have told that the swallows had started rebuilding their nest.

o'clock; I will go and see if my swallows are on their nest. Yes! there they are, side by side, both looking down into the garden. I have been out on purpose to see their faces. I knew by looking at the window that they were there. Young George Mackareth is come down from London. Molly says: "I did not get him asked if he had got his la'al green purse yet". When he went away he went round to see aw't neighbours and some gave him 6d., some a shilling, and I have heard his Mother say "'t la'al green purse was never out of his hand". I wrote to M. H., my brother Christr. and Miss Griffith, then went to bed in the sitting room. C. and Wm. came in at about half-past eleven. They talked till after twelve.

June 30th, Wednesday. William slept ill, his head terribly bad. We walked part of the way up the Rays with Coleridge, a threatening windy coldish day. We did not go with C. far up the Rays, but sate down a few minutes together before we parted. I was not very well — I was inclined to go to bed when we reached home, but Wm. persuaded me to have tea instead. We met an old man between the [?] shed and Lewthwaite's. He wore a rusty but untorn hat, an excellent blue coat, waistcoat, and breeches, and good mottled worsted stockings. His beard was very thick and grey, of a fortnight's growth we guessed, it was a regular beard, like grey *plush*. His bundle contained Sheffield ware. William said to him, after he had asked him what his business was, "You are a very old man?" "Aye, I am 83." I joined in, "Have you any children?" "Children? Yes, plenty. I have children and grand-children, and great grand-children. I have a great grand-daughter, a fine lass, 13 years old." I then said, "What, they take care of you?" He replied, half offended, "Thank God, I can take care of myself". He said he had been a servant of the Marquis of Granby — "O he was a good man, he's in heaven — I hope he is". He then told us how he shot himself at Bath, that he was with him in Germany, and travelled with him everywhere. "He was a famous boxer, sir." And then he told us a story of his fighting with his farmer. "He used always to call me hard and sharp." Then every now and then he broke out, "He was a good man! When we were travelling he never asked at the public-houses, as it might be there" (pointing to the "Swan"), "what we were to pay, but he would put his hand into his pocket and give them what he liked; and when he came out of the house he would say, Now, they would have charged me a shilling or tenpence. God help them, poor creatures!!" I asked him again about his children, how many he had. Says he, "I cannot tell you" (I suppose he confounded children and grand-children together); "I have one daughter that keeps a boarding-school at Skipton in Craven. She teaches flowering and marking. And another that keeps a boarding-school at Ingleton. I brought up my family under the Marquis." He was familiar with all parts of Yorkshire. He asked us where we lived. "At Grasmere." "The bonniest dale in England!" says the old man. I bought a pair of scissors of him, and we sate together by the road-side. When we parted I tried to lift his

Dame School, Elterwater, by John Harden

bundle, and it was almost more than I could do. We got tea and I was somewhat better. After tea I wrote to Coleridge, and closed up my letter to M. H. We went soon to bed. A weight of children a poor man's blessing. I [?] myself.

July 1st, Thursday. A very rainy day. We did not go out at all, till evening. I laid down after dinner, but first we sate quietly together by the fire. In the evening we took my cloak and walked first to the top of White Moss, then round by the White Bridge, and up again beyond Mr. Olliff's — we had a nice walk, and afterwards sate by a nice snug fire, and William read Spenser, and I read *As you like it.* The saddle bags came from Keswick, with a letter from M. H. and from C., and Wilkinson's drawings, but no letter from Richard.

July 2nd, Friday. A very rainy morning. There was a gleam of fair weather, and we thought of walking into Easedale. Molly began to prepare the linen for putting out, but it rained worse than ever. In the evening we walked up to the view of Rydale, and afterwards towards Mr. King's. I left William, and wrote a short letter to M. H. and to Coleridge, and transcribed the alterations in *The Leech Gatherer.*

July 3rd, Saturday. I breakfasted in bed, being not very well. Aggy Ashburner helped Molly with the linen. I made veal and gooseberry pies. It was very cold. Thomas Ashburner went for coals for us. There was snow upon the mountain tops. Letters from M. H. and Annette — A.'s letter sent from G. Hill — written at Blois 23rd.

July 4th, Sunday. Cold and rain and very dark. I was sick and ill, had been made sleepless by letters. I lay in bed till 4 o'clock. When I rose, I was very far from well, but I grew better after tea. William walked out a little, I did not. We sate at the window together. It came on a terribly wet night. Wm. finished *The Leech Gatherer* today.

July 5th, Monday. A very sweet morning. William stayed some time in the orchard. I went to him there — it was a beautiful morning. I copied out *The L.-G.* for Coleridge, and for us. Wrote to Annette, — Mrs. Clarkson, M. H., and Coleridge. It came on a heavy rain, and we could not go to Dove Nest as we had intended, though we had sent Molly for the horse, and it was come. The roses in the garden are fretted and battered and quite spoiled, the honey suckle, though in its glory, is sadly teazed. The peas are beaten down. The scarlet beans want sticking. The garden is overrun with weeds.

July 6th, Tuesday. It was a very rainy day, but in the afternoon it cleared up a little and we set off towards Rydale to go for letters. The rain met us at the top of the White Moss, and it came on very heavily afterwards. It drove past Nab Scar in a substantial shape, as if going Grasmere-wards as fast as it could go. We stopped at Willy Park's and borrowed a plaid. I rested a little while till the rain seemed passing away, and then I went to meet William. I met him near Rydale with a letter from Christopher. We had a pleasant but very rainy walk home. A letter came from Mary in the morning, and in the evening one from Coleridge by Fletcher. The swallows have completed their beautiful nest. I baked bread and pies.

[*July*] *7th, Wednesday.* A very fine day. William had slept ill, so he lay in bed till 11 o'clock. I wrote to John, ironed the linen, packed up. Lay in the orchard all the afternoon. In the morning Wm. nailed up the trees while I was ironing. We lay sweetly in the orchard. The well is beautiful. The orchard full of foxgloves. The honeysuckle beautiful — plenty of roses, but they are battered. Wrote to Molly Ritson [?] and Coleridge. Walked on the White Moss. Glow-worms. Well for them children are in bed when they shine.

[*July*] *8th, Thursday.* A rainy morning. I paid Thomas Ashburner and Frank Baty. When I was coming home, a post-chaise passed with a little girl behind in a patched, ragged red cloak [?]. We sat in tranquillity together by the fire in the morning. In the afternoon, after we had talked a little, William fell asleep. I read the *Winter's Tale*; then I went to bed, but did not sleep. The swallows stole in and out of their nest, and sate there, *whiles* quite still, *whiles* they sung low for two minutes or more at a time just like a muffled robin. William was looking at *The Pedlar* when I got up. He arranged it, and after tea I wrote it out — 280 lines. In the meantime the evening being fine he carried his coat to the tailor's, and went to George Mackareth's to engage the horse. He came in to me at about ½ past nine pressing me to go out; he had got letters which we were to read out of doors — I was rather unwilling, fearing I could not see to read the letters, but I saw well enough. One was from M. H., a very tender affecting letter, another from Sara to C., from C. to us, and from my Br. Rd. The moon was behind. William hurried me out in hopes that I should see her. We walked first to the top of the hill to see Rydale. It was dark and dull, but our own vale was very solemn — the shape of Helm Crag was quite distinct, though black. We walked backwards and forwards on the White Moss path; there was a sky-like white brightness on the lake. The Wyke cottage light at the foot of Silver How. Glow-worms out, but not so numerous as last night. O, beautiful place! Dear Mary, William. The horse is come — Friday morning — so I must give over. William is eating his broth. I

Skiddaw: Summer Evening with a Stage Coach, by P. J. de Loutherbourg

must prepare to go. The swallows, I must leave them, the well, the garden, the roses, all. Dear creatures!! they sang last night after I was in bed — seemed to be singing to one another, just before they settled to rest for the night. Well, I must go. Farewell.

On Friday morning, July 9th, William and I set forward to Keswick on our road to Gallow Hill. We had a pleasant ride, though the day was showery. It rained heavily when Nelly Mackareth took the horse from us, at the Black-smith's. Coleridge met us at Sara's Rock. He had inquired about us before of Nelly Mackareth and we had been told by a handsome man, an inhabitant of Wytheburn, with whom he had been talking (and who seemed, by the bye, much pleased with his companion), that C. was waiting for us. We reached Keswick against tea-time. We called at Calvert's on the Saturday evening. On Sunday I was poorly and the day was wet, so we could not move from Keswick, but on Monday 12th July 1802 we went to Eusemere. Coleridge walked with us 6 or 7 miles. He was not well, and we had a melancholy parting after having sate together in silence by the road-side. We turned aside to explore the country near Hutton-John, and had a new and delightful walk. The valley, which is subject to the decaying mansion that stands at its head, seems to join its testimony to that of the house to the falling away of the family greatness. The hedges are in bad condition, the land wants draining, and is overrun with brackens, yet there is a something everywhere that tells of its former possessors. The trees are left scattered about as if intended to be like a park, and these are very interesting, standing as they do upon the sides of the steep hills that slope down to the bed of the river, a little stony-bedded stream that spreads out to a considerable breadth at the village of Dacre. A little above Dacre we came into the right road to Mr. Clarkson's, after having walked through woods and fields, never exactly know-ing whether we were right or wrong. We learnt, however, that we had saved half-a-mile. We sate down by the river-side to rest, and saw some swallows flying about and about under the bridge, and two little schoolboys were loitering among the scars seeking after their nests. We reached Mr. Clarkson's at about eight o'clock after a sauntering walk, having lingered and loitered and sate down together that we might be alone. Mr. and Mrs. C. were just come from Luff's.

We spent Tuesday, the 13th of July, at Eusemere; and on Wednesday morning, the 14th, we walked to Emont Bridge, and mounted the coach between Bird's Nest and Hartshorn Tree. Mr. Clarkson's bitch followed us so far. A soldier and his young wife wanted to be taken up by that Coachman, but there was no room. We had a chearful ride though cold till we got on to Stainmoor, and then a heavy shower came on, but we buttoned ourselves up both together in the Guard's coat, and we liked the hills and the rain the better for bringing us so close to one another — I never rode more snugly. At last however it grew so very rainy that I was obliged to go into the coach at Bowes. Lough of Penrith was there and very impertinent — I was right glad to get out again to my own dear Brother at Greta Bridge; the sun shone chearfully, and a glorious ride we had over Gaterly Moor. Every building was bathed in golden light. The trees were more bright than earthly trees, and we saw round us miles beyond miles — Darlington spire, etc. etc. We reached Leeming Lane at about 9 o'clock: supped comfortably, and enjoyed our fire.

On Thursday morning, at a little before seven, being the 15th July, we got into a post-chaise and went to Thirsk to breakfast. We were well treated, but when the landlady understood that we were going to *walk* off, and leave our luggage behind, she threw out some saucy words in our hearing. The day was very hot, and we rested often and long before we reached the foot of the Hambledon Hills, and while we were climbing them, still oftener. We had a sandwich in our pockets which we finished when we had climbed part of the hill, and we were almost overpowered with thirst, when I heard the trickling of a little stream of water. I was before William, and I stopped till he came up to me. We sate a long time by this water, and climbed the hill slowly. I was footsore, the sun shone hot, the little Scotch cattle panted and tossed fretfully about. The view was hazy, and we could see nothing from the top of the hill but an indistinct wide-spreading country, full of trees, but the buildings, towns, and houses were lost. We stopped to examine that curious stone, then walked along the flat common. It was now cooler, but I was still footsore and could not walk quick, so I left William sitting two or three times, and when he followed me he took a sheep for me, and then me for a sheep. I rested opposite the Sign of the Sportsman and was questioned by the Landlady.

Arrived very hungry at Rivaux. Nothing to eat at the Millers, as we expected, but at an exquisitely neat farmhouse we got some boiled milk and bread; this strengthened us, and I went down to look at the ruins. Thrushes were singing, cattle feeding among green-grown hillocks about the ruins. These hillocks were scattered over with *grovelets* of wild roses and other shrubs, and covered with wild flowers. I could have stayed in this solemn quiet spot till evening, without a thought of moving, but William was waiting for me, so in a quarter of an hour I went away. We walked upon Mr. Duncombe's terrace and looked down upon the Abbey. It stands in a larger valley among a brotherhood of valleys, of different length and breadth, — all woody, and running up into the hills in different directions. We reached Helmsly just at dusk. We had a beautiful view of the castle from the top of the hill, slept at a very nice inn, and were well treated — bright bellows and floors as smooth as ice. On Friday morning, 16th July, we walked to Kirby. Met people coming to Helmsly fair. Were misdirected, and walked a mile out of our way — met a double horse at Kirby. A beautiful view above Pickering — Sinnington village very beautiful. Met Mary and Sara seven miles from G. H. Sheltered from the rain; beautiful glen, spoiled by the large house — sweet church and churchyard. Arrived at Gallow Hill at 7 o'clock.

July 16th, Friday Evening. The weather bad, almost all the time. Sara, Tom, and I rode up Bedale. Wm., Mary, Sara, and I went to Scarborough, and we walked in the Abbey pasture, and to Wykeham; and on Monday, the 26th, we went off with Mary in a post-chaise. We had an interesting ride over the Wolds, though it rained all the way. Single thorn bushes were scattered about on the turf, sheepsheds here and there, and now and then a little hut. Swelling grounds, and sometimes a single tree or a clump of trees. Mary was very sick, and every time we stopped to open a gate she felt the motion in her whole body — indeed I was sick too, and perhaps the smooth gliding of the chaise over the turf made us worse. We passed through one or two little villages, embosomed in tall trees. After we had parted from Mary, there were gleams of sunshine, but with showers. We saw Beverley in a heavy rain, and yet were much pleased with the beauty of the town. Saw the Minster — a pretty, clean building, but injured very much with Grecian architecture. The country between Beverley and Hull very rich, but miserably flat — brick houses, windmills, houses again — dull and endless. Hull a frightful, dirty, *brick-housey,* tradesmanlike, rich, vulgar place; yet the river, though the shores are so low that they can hardly be seen, looked beautiful with the evening lights upon it, and boats moving about. We walked a long time, and returned to our dull day-room but quiet evening one, quiet and our own, to supper.

July 27th, Tuesday. Market day. Streets dirty, very rainy, did not leave Hull till 4 o'clock, and left Barton at about six; rained all the way almost. A beautiful village at the foot of a hill with trees. A gentleman's house converted into a lady's boarding-school. We had a woman in bad health in the coach, and took in a lady and her daughter — supped at Lincoln, duck and peas, and cream cheese — paid 2/-. We left Lincoln on Wednesday morning, 28th July, at six o'clock. It rained

Stage Coach at Lincoln, by J. M. W. Turner

heavily, and we could see nothing but the antientry of some of the buildings as we passed along. The night before, however, we had seen enough to make us regret this. The minster stands at the edge of a hill overlooking an immense plain. The country very flat as we went along — the day mended. We went to see the outside of the Minster while the passengers were dining at Peterborough; the West End very grand. The little girl, who was a great scholar and plainly her Mother's favourite, though she had a large family at home, had bought "The Farmer's Boy". She said it was written by a man without education and was very wonderful.

On Thursday morning, 29th, we arrived in London. Wm. left me at the Inn. I went to bed, etc. etc. After various troubles and disasters, we left London on Saturday morning at ½-past 5 or 6, the 31st of July. (I have forgot which.) We mounted the Dover Coach at Charing Cross. It was a beautiful morning. The city, St. Paul's, with the river and a multitude of little boats, made a most beautiful sight, as we crossed Westminster Bridge. The houses were not over-hung by their cloud of smoke, and they were spread out endlessly, yet the sun shone so brightly, with such a fierce light, that there was even something like the purity of one of nature's own grand spectacles.

We rode on chearfully, now with the Paris diligence before us, now behind. We walked up the steep hills, a beautiful prospect everywhere, till we even reached Dover. At first the rich, populous, wide-spreading, woody country about Lon-don, then the River Thames, ships sailing, chalk-cliffs, trees, little villages. Afterwards Canterbury, situated on a plain, rich and woody, but the City and Cathedral disappointed me. Hop grounds on each side of the road some miles from Canterbury, then we came to a common, the race ground, an elevated plain, villages among trees in the bed of a valley at our right, and, rising above this valley, green hills scattered over with wood, neat gentlemen's houses. One white house, almost hid with green trees, which we longed for, and the parson's house, as neat a place as could be, which would just have suited Coleridge. No doubt we might have found one for Tom Hutchinson and Sara, and a good farm too. We halted at a half-way house — fruit carts under the shade of trees, seats for guests, a tempting place to the weary traveller. Still, as we went along, the country was beautiful, hilly, with cottages lurking under the hills, and their little plots of hop ground like vineyards. It was a bad hop year. A woman on the top of the coach said to me, "It is a sad thing for the poor people, for the hop-gathering is the women's harvest; there is employment about the hops both for women and children".

We saw the castle of Dover, and the sea beyond, 4 or 5 miles before we reached D. We looked at it through a long vale, the castle being upon an eminence, as it seemed, at the end of this vale, which opened to the sea. The country now became less fertile, but near Dover it seemed more rich again. Many buildings stand on the flat fields, sheltered with tall trees. There is one old chapel that might have been there just in the same state in which it now is when this vale was as retired, and as little known to travellers as our own Cumberland mountain wilds 30 years

SONNET COMPOSED UPON WESTMINSTER
BRIDGE, SEPTEMBER 3, 1802

Earth has not anything to show more fair:
Dull would he be of soul who could pass by
A sight so touching in its majesty:
This City now doth, like a garment, wear
The beauty of the morning; silent, bare,
Ships, towers, domes, theatres, and temples lie
Open unto the fields, and to the sky;
All bright and glittering in the smokeless air.
Never did sun more beautifully steep
In his first splendour, valley, rock, or hill;
Ne'er saw I, never felt, a calm so deep!
The river glideth at his own sweet will:
Dear God! the very houses seem asleep;
And all that mighty heart is lying still!

William Wordsworth

The Evening Coach, London from Greenwich, by P. J. de Loutherbourg

ago. There was also a very old building on the other side of the road, which had a strange effect among the many new ones that are springing up everywhere. It seemed odd that it could have kept itself pure in its ancientry among so many upstarts. It was near dark when we reached Dover. We were told that the packet was about to sail, so we went down to the custom-house in half-an-hour — had our luggage examined, etc. etc., and then we drank tea with the Honourable Mr. Knox and his tutor. We arrived at Calais at 4 o'clock on Sunday morning, the 1st of August. We stayed in the vessel till ½-past 7, then William went for letters, at about ½-past 8 or 9 we found out Annette and C. chez Madame Avril dans la Rue de la Tête d'or. We lodged opposite two ladies, in tolerably decent-sized rooms, but badly furnished and with large store and bad smells and dirt in the yard, and all about. The weather was very hot. We walked by the seaside almost every evening with Annette and Caroline, or Wm. and I alone. I had a bad cold, and could not bathe at first, but William did. It was a pretty sight to see, as we walked upon the sands when the tide was low, perhaps a hundred people bathing about a quarter of a mile distant from us, and we had delightful walks after the heat of the day was passed away — seeing far off in the west the coast of England like a cloud crested with Dover Castle, which was but like the summit of the cloud — the evening star and the glory of the sky. The reflections in the water were more beautiful than the sky itself, purple waves brighter than precious stones, for ever melting away upon the sands. The fort, a wooden building, at the entrance of the harbour at Calais, when the evening twilight was coming on, and we could not

The Beach at Dover

see anything of the building but its shape, which was far more distinct than in perfect daylight, seemed to be reared upon pillars of ebony, between which pillars the sea was seen in the most beautiful colours that can be conceived. Nothing in romance was ever half so beautiful. Now came in view, as the evening star sank down, and the colours of the west faded away, the two lights of England, lighted up by Englishmen in our country, to warn vessels off rocks or sands. These we used to see from the pier, when we could see no other distant objects but the clouds, the sky, and the sea itself: All was dark behind. The town of Calais seemed deserted of the light of heaven, but there was always light and life and joy upon the sea. One night, though, I shall never forget — the day had been very hot, and William and I walked alone together upon the pier. The sea was gloomy, for there was a blackness over all the sky, except when it was overspread with lightning, which often revealed to us a distant vessel. Near us the waves roared and broke against the pier, and they were interfused with greenish fiery light. The more distant sea always black and gloomy. It was also beautiful, on the calm hot night, to see the little boats row out of harbour with wings of fire, and the sail boats with the fiery track which they cut as they went along, and which closed up after them with a hundred thousand sparkles, balls, shootings and streams of glow-worm light. Caroline was delighted.

On Sunday, the 29th of August, we left Calais at twelve o'clock in the morning, and landed at Dover at one on Monday the 30th. I was sick all the way. It was very pleasant to me, when we were in harbour at Dover, to breathe the

Brompton Church (where William Wordsworth and Mary Hutchinson were married)

fresh air, and to look up and see the stars among the ropes of the vessel. The next day was very hot. We both bathed, and sate upon the Dover Cliffs, and looked upon France with many a melancholy and tender thought. We could see the shores almost as plain as if it were but an English lake. We mounted the coach at ½ past 4, and arrived in London at 6, the 30th August. It was misty, and we could see nothing. We stayed in London till Wednesday the 22nd of September, and arrived at Gallow Hill on Friday.

[*Friday*], *September 24th*. Mary first met us in the avenue. She looked so fat and well that we were made very happy by the sight of her; then came Sara, and last of all Joanna. Tom was forking corn, standing upon the corn cart. We dressed ourselves immediately and got tea — the garden looked gay with asters and sweet peas. Jack and George came on Friday evening, 1st October. On Saturday, 2nd, we rode to Hackness, William, Jack, George, and Sara single — I behind Tom. On Sunday 3rd, Mary and Sara were busy packing.

On Monday, 4th October 1802, my brother William was married to Mary Hutchinson. I slept a good deal of the night, and rose fresh and well in the morning. At a little after 8 o'clock I saw them go down the avenue towards the church. William had parted from me upstairs. When they were absent my dear little Sara prepared the breakfast. I kept myself as quiet as I could, but when I saw the two men running up the walk, coming to tell us it was over, I could stand it no longer, and threw myself on the bed, where I lay in stillness, neither hearing or seeing anything till Sara came upstairs to me, and said, "They are coming". This forced me from the bed where I lay, and I moved, I knew not how, straight forward, faster than my strength could carry me, till I met my beloved William, and fell upon his bosom. He and John Hutchinson led me to the house, and there I stayed to welcome my dear Mary. As soon as we had breakfasted, we departed. It rained when we set off. Poor Mary was much agitated, when she parted from her brothers and sisters, and her home. Nothing particular occurred till we reached Kirby. We had sunshine and showers, pleasant talk, love and chearfulness. We were obliged to stay two hours at K. while the horses were feeding. We wrote a few lines to Sara, and then walked out; the sun shone, and we went to the churchyard after we had put a letter into the post-office for the *York Herald*. We sauntered about, and read the grave-stones. There was one to the memory of five children, who had all died within five years, and the longest lived had only lived four years. There was another stone erected to the memory of an unfortunate woman (as we supposed, by a stranger). The verses engraved upon it expressed that she had been neglected by her relations, and counselled the readers of those words to look within, and recollect their own frailties. We left Kirby at about half-past two. There is not much variety of prospect from K. to Helmsley, but the country is very pleasant, being rich and woody, and Helmsley itself stands very sweetly at the foot of the rising grounds of Duncombe Park, which is scattered over with tall woods; and, lifting itself above the common buildings of the town, stands Helmsley Castle, now a ruin, formerly inhabited by the gay Duke of Buckingham. Every foot of the road was, of itself, interesting to us, for we had travelled along it on foot, Wm. and I, when we went to fetch our dear Mary, and had sate upon the turf by the roadside more than once. Before we reached Helmsley, our driver told us that he could not take us any further, so we stopped at the same inn where we had slept before. My heart danced at the sight of its cleanly outside, bright yellow walls, casements overshadowed with jasmine, and its low, double gavel-ended front. We were not shown into the same parlour where Wm. and I were; it was a small room with a drawing over the chimney piece which the woman told us had been bought at a sale. Mary and I warmed ourselves at the kitchen fire. We then walked into the garden, and looked over a gate, up to the old ruin which stands at the top of a mount, and round about it the moats are grown up into soft green cradles, hollows surrounded with green grassy hillocks, and these are overshadowed by old trees, chiefly ashes. I prevailed upon William to go up with me to the ruins. We left Mary sitting by the kitchen fire. The sun shone, it was warm and very pleasant. One part of the castle seems to be inhabited. There was a man mowing nettles in the open space which had most likely once been the castle-court. There is one gateway exceedingly beautiful. Children were playing upon the sloping ground. We came home by the street. After about an hour's delay we set forward again, had an excellent driver, who opened the gates so dexterously that the horses never stopped. Mary was very much delighted with the view of the castle from the point where we had seen it before. I was pleased to see again the little path which we had walked upon, the gate I had climbed over, and the road down which we had seen the two little boys drag a log of wood, and a team of horses struggle under the weight of a great load of timber. We had felt compassion for the poor horses that were under the governance of oppressive and ill-judging drivers, and for the poor boys, who seemed of an age to have been able to have dragged the log of wood merely out of the love of their own activity, but from poverty and bad food they panted for weakness, and were obliged to fetch their father from the town to help them. Duncombe House looks well from the road — a large building, though I believe only two-thirds of the original designs are completed. We rode down a very steep hill to Rivaux valley, with woods all around us. We stopped upon the bridge to look at the Abbey, and again when we had crossed it. Dear Mary had never seen a ruined abbey before except Whitby. We recognised the cottages, houses, and the little valleys as we went along. We walked up a long hill, the road carrying us up the cleft or valley with woody hills on each side of us. When we went to G. H. I had walked down the valley alone. William followed me.

It was not dark evening when we passed the little publick house, but before we had crossed the Hambledon Hill, and reached the point overlooking Yorkshire, it was quite dark. We had not wanted, however, fair prospects before us, as we drove along the flat plain of the high hill. Far far off us, in the western sky, we saw shapes of castles, ruins among groves, a great spreading wood, rocks, and single trees, a minster with its tower unusually distinct, minarets in another quarter, and a round Grecian Temple also; the colours of the sky of a bright grey,

Rievaulx Abbey, by John Sell Cotman

and the forms of a sober grey, with a dome. As we descended the hill there was no distinct view, but of a great space; only near us we saw the wild and (as the people say) bottomless tarn in the hollow at the side of the hill. It seemed to be made visible to us only by its own light, for all the hill about us was dark. Before we reached Thirsk we saw a light before us, which we at first thought was the moon, then lime-kilns; but when we drove into the market-place it proved a large bonfire, with lads dancing round it, which is a sight I dearly love. The inn was like an illuminated house — every room full. We asked the cause, and were told by the girl that it was "Mr. John Bell's birthday, that he had heired his estate!" The landlady was very civil. She did not recognise the despised foot-travellers. We rode nicely in the dark, and reached Leeming Lane at eleven o'clock. I am always sorry to get out of a chaise when it is night. The people of the house were going to bed and we were not very well treated, though we got a hot supper. We breakfasted next morning and set off at about ½-past 8 o'clock. It was a chearful, sunny morning. We soon turned out of Leeming Lane and passed a nice village with a beautiful church. We had a few showers, but when we came to the green fields of Wensley, the sun shone upon them all, and the Ure in its many windings glittered as it flowed along under the green slopes of Middleham and Middleham Castle. Mary looked about for her friend Mr. Place, and thought she had him sure on the contrary side of the vale from that on which we afterwards found that he lived. We went to a new built house at Leyburn, the same village where William and I had dined with George Hutchinson on our road to Grasmere 2 years and ¾ ago, but not the same house. The landlady was very civil, giving us cake and wine, but the horses being out we were detained at least two hours, and did not set off till 2 o'clock. We paid for 35 miles, *i.e.* to Sedbergh, but the landlady did not encourage us to hope to get beyond Hawes. A shower came on just after we left the inn — while the rain beat against the windows we ate our dinners, which M. and W. heartily enjoyed — I was not quite well. When we passed through the village of Wensley my heart was melted away with dear recollections — the bridge, the little waterspout, the steep hill, the church. They are among the most vivid of my own inner visions, for they were the first objects that I saw after we were left to ourselves, and had turned our whole hearts to Grasmere as a home in which we were to rest. The vale looked most beautiful each way. To the left the bright silver stream inlaid the flat and very green meadows, winding like a serpent. To the right we did not see it so far, it was lost among trees and little hills. I could not help observing, as we went along, how much more varied the prospects of Wensley Dale are in the summer time than I could have thought possible in the winter. This seemed to be in great measure owing to the trees being in leaf, and forming groves and screens, and thence little openings upon recesses and concealed retreats, which in winter only made a part of the one great vale. The *beauty* of the summer time here as much excels that of the winter, as the variety, owing to the excessive greenness of the fields, and the trees in leaf half concealing, and, where they do not conceal, softening the hard bareness of the limey white roofs. One of our horses seemed to grow a little restive as we went

through the first village, a long village on the side of a hill. It grew worse and worse, and at last we durst not go on any longer. We walked a while, and then the post boy was obliged to take the horse out, and go back for another. We seated ourselves again snugly in the Post Chaise. The wind struggled about us and rattled the window, and gave a gentle motion to the chaise, but we were warm and at our ease within. Our station was at the top of a hill, opposite Bolton Castle, the Ure flowing beneath. William has since wrote a sonnet on this our imprisonment. "Hard was thy durance, Queen! compared with ours." Poor Mary!

Wm. fell asleep, lying upon my breast, and I upon Mary. I lay motionless for a long time, but I was at last obliged to move. I became very sick and continued so for some time after the boy brought the horse to us. Mary had been a little sick, but it soon went off. We had a sweet ride till we came to a publick-house on the side of a hill, where we alighted and walked down to see the waterfalls. The sun was not set, and the woods and fields were spread over with the yellow light of evening, which made their greenness a thousand times more green. There was too much water in the river for the beauty of the falls, and even the banks were less interesting than in winter. Nature had entirely got the better in her struggles against the giants who first cast the mould of these works; for, indeed, it is a place that did not in winter remind one of God, but one could not help feeling as if there had been the agency of some "mortal instruments", which Nature had been struggling against without making a perfect conquest. There was something so wild and new in this feeling, knowing, as we did in the inner man, that God alone had laid his hand upon it, that I could not help regretting the want of it; besides, it is a pleasure to a real lover of Nature to give winter all the glory he can, for

Market Day,

by W. H. Pyne

summer *will* make its own way, and speak its own praises. We saw the pathway which William and I took at the close of evening, the path leading to the rabbit warren where we lost ourselves. The farm, with its holly hedges, was lost among the green hills and hedgerows in general, but we found it out, and were glad to look at it again. When William had left us to seek the waterfalls, Mary and I were frightened by a cow.

At our return to the inn, we found new horses and a new driver, and we went on nicely to Hawes, where we arrived before it was quite dark. Mary and I got tea and William had a partridge and mutton chops and tarts for his supper. Mary sate down with him. We also had a shilling's worth of negus, and Mary made me some broth, for all which supper we were only charged 2/-. I could not sit up long, I vomited and took the broth and then slept sweetly. We rose at six o'clock — a rainy morning. We had a good breakfast and then departed. There was a very pretty view about a mile from Hawes, where we crossed a bridge; bare and very green fields with cattle, a glittering stream, cottages, a few ill-grown trees, and high hills. The sun shone now. Before we got upon the bare hills, there was a hunting lodge on our right, exactly like Greta Hill, with fir plantations about it. We were very fortunate in the day, gleams of sunshine, passing clouds, that travelled with their shadows below them. Mary was much pleased with Garsdale. It was a dear place to William and me. We noted well the publick-house (Garsdale Hall) where we had baited, and drunk our pint of ale, and afterwards the mountain which had been adorned by Jupiter in his glory when we were here before. It was mid-day when we reached Sedbergh, and *market* day. We were in the same room where we had spent the evening together in our road to Grasmere. We had a pleasant ride to Kendal, where we arrived at about 2 o'clock. The day favoured us. M. and I went to see the house where dear Sara had lived, then we went to seek Mr. Bonsfield's shop, but we found him not. He had sold all his goods the day before. We then went to the Pot-woman's and bought 2 jugs and a dish, and some paper at Pennington's. When we came to the Inn William was almost ready for us. The afternoon was not chearful but it did not rain till we came near Windermere. I am always glad to see Stavely; it is a place I dearly love to think of — the first mountain village that I came to with Wm. when we first began our pilgrimage together. Here we drank a bason of milk at a publick house, and here I washed my feet in the brook, and put on a pair of silk stockings by Wm.'s advice. Nothing particular occurred till we reached Ings chapel. The door was open, and we went in. It is a neat little place, with a marble floor and marble communion table, with a painting over it of the last supper, and Moses and Aaron on each side. The woman told us that "they had painted them as near as they could by the dresses as they are described in the Bible", and gay enough they are. The marble had been sent by Richard Bateman from Leghorn. The woman told us that a man had been at her house a few days before, who told her he had helped to bring it down the Red Sea, and she had believed him gladly! It rained very hard when we reached Windermere. We sate in the rain at Wilcock's to change horses and arrived at Grasmere at about 6 o'clock on Wednesday evening, the 6th of

Group at Brathay Hall, by John Harden

October 1802. Molly was overjoyed to see us, for my part I cannot describe what I felt, and our dear Mary's feelings would I dare say not be easy to speak of. We went by candle light into the garden, and were astonished at the growth of the brooms, Portugal laurels, etc. etc. etc. The next day, Thursday, we unpacked the boxes. On Friday, 8th, we baked bread and Mary and I walked, first upon the hill-side, and then in John's Grove, then in view of Rydale, the first walk that I had taken with my sister.

[*October*] 9*th, Saturday*. William and I walked to Mr. Simpson's.

[*October*] 10*th, Sunday*. Rain all day.

[*October*] 11*th, Monday*. A beautiful day. We walked to the Easedale hills to hunt waterfalls. William and Mary left me sitting on a stone on the solitary mountains, and went to Easedale tarn. I grew chilly and followed them. This approach to the tarn is very beautiful. We expected to have found C. at home, but he did not come till after dinner. He was well, but did not look so.

October 12*th, Tuesday*. We walked with C. to Rydale.

[*October*] 13*th, Wednesday*. Set forwards with him towards Keswick, and he prevailed us to go on. We consented, Mrs. C. not being at home. The day was delightful. We drank tea at John Stanley's. Wrote to Annette.

[*October*] 14*th, Thursday*. We went in the evening to Calvert's. Moonlight. Stayed supper.

[*October*] 15*th, Friday*. Walked to Lord William Gordon's.

[*October*] 16*th, Saturday*. Came home, Mary and I. William returned to Coleridge before we reached Nadel Fell. Mary and I had a pleasant walk, the day was very bright; the people busy getting in their corn, reached home at about five o'clock. I was not quite well, but better after tea. We made cakes etc.

[*October*] 17*th, Sunday*. We had thirteen of our neighbours to tea. William came in just as we began tea.

[*October*] 18*th, Monday*. I was not very well. I walked up in the morning to the Simpsons.

[*October*] 19*th, Tuesday*. The Simpsons drank tea and supped. William was much oppressed.

[*October*] 20*th, Wednesday*. We all walked on Butterlip How. It rained.

[*October*] 21*st, Thursday*. I walked with William to Rydale.

[*October*] 22*nd, Friday*.

[*October*] 23*rd, Saturday*. Mary was baking. I walked with Wm. to see Langdale, Rydale and the foot of Grasmere. We had a heavenly walk, but I came home in the toothache and have since that day been confined upstairs till now, namely, *Saturday*, 30th October, 1802.

October 30th, Saturday. William is gone to Keswick. Mary went with him to the top of the Rays. She is returned, and is now sitting near me by the fire. It is a breathless, grey day, that leaves the golden woods of autumn quiet in their own tranquillity, stately and beautiful in their decaying; the lake is a perfect mirror.

William met Stoddart at the bridge at the foot of Legberthwaite dale. He returned with him and they surprized us by their arrival at four o'clock in the afternoon. Stoddart and W. dined. I went to bed, and after tea S. read Chaucer to us.

October 31st, Sunday. John Monkhouse called. William and S. went to K[eswick]. Mary and I walked to the top of the hill and looked at Rydale. I was much affected when I stood upon the second bar of Sara's gate. The lake was perfectly still, the sun shone on hill and vale, the distant birch trees looked like large golden flowers. Nothing else in colour was distinct and separate, but all the beautiful colours seemed to be melted into one another, and joined together in one mass, so that there were no differences, though an endless variety, when one tried to find it out. The fields were of one sober yellow brown. After dinner we both lay on the floor — Mary slept. I could not for I was thinking of so many things. We sate nicely together after tea looking over old letters. Molly was gone up to Mr. Simpson's to see Mrs. S. who was very ill.

November 1st, Monday. I wrote to Miss Lamb. After dinner Mary walked to Mr. Simpson's. Letters from Cook, Wrangham, Mrs. C.

November 2nd, Tuesday. William returned from K. — he was not well. Baking day. Mr. B. S. came in at tea time. Molly sate up with Mrs. S. William was not well this evening.

[*November*] *3rd, Wednesday*. Mr. Luff came in to tea.

[*November*] *4th, Thursday*. I scalded my foot with coffee after having been in bed in the afternoon — I was near fainting and then bad in my bowels. Mary waited upon me till 2 o'clock, then we went to bed, and with applications of vinegar I was lulled to sleep about 4.

[*November*] *5th, Friday*. I was laid up all day. I wrote to Montagu and Cook, and sent off letters to Miss Lamb and Coleridge.

[*November*] *6th, Saturday*.

[*November*] *7th, Sunday*. Fine weather. Letters from Coleridge that he was gone to London. Sara at Penrith. I wrote to Mrs. Clarkson. Wm. began to translate Ariosto.

[*November*] *8th, Monday*. A beautiful day. William got to work again at Ariosto, and so continued all the morning, though the day was so delightful that it made my very heart linger to be out of doors, and see and feel the beauty of the autumn in freedom. The trees on the opposite side of the lake are of a yellow brown, but there are one or two trees opposite our windows (an ash tree, for instance) quite green, as in spring. The fields are of their winter colour, but the island is as green as ever it was. Mary has been baking today, she is now sitting in the parlour. William is writing out his stanzas from Ariosto. We have a nice fire — the evening is quiet. Poor Coleridge! Sara is at Keswick, I hope. William has been ill

in his stomach, but he is better tonight. I have read one canto of Ariosto today.

December 24th, Christmas Eve. William is now sitting by me, at ½ past 10 o'clock. I have been beside him ever since tea running the heel of a stocking, repeating some of his sonnets to him, listening to his own repeating, reading some of Milton's, and the *Allegro* and *Penseroso.* It is a quiet keen frost. Mary is in the parlour below attending to the baking of cakes, and Jenny Fletcher's pies. Sara is in bed in the toothache, and so we are [?]. My beloved William is turning over the leaves of Charlotte Smith's sonnets, but he keeps his hand to his poor chest, pushing aside his breastplate. Mary is well and I am well, and Molly is as blithe as last year at this time. Coleridge came this morning with Wedgwood. We all turned out of Wm.'s bedroom one by one, to meet him. He looked well. We had to tell him of the birth of his little girl, born yesterday morning at 6 o'clock. Wm. went with them to Wytheburn in the chaise, and M. and I met W. on the Rays. It was not an unpleasant morning to the feeling! far from it. The sun shone now and then, and there was no wind, but all things looked chearless and distinct; no meltings of sky into mountains, the mountains like stone work wrought up with huge hammers. Last Sunday was as mild a day as I ever remember. We all set off together to walk. I went to Rydale and Wm. returned with me. M. and S. went round the lakes. There were flowers of various kinds — the topmost bell of a foxglove, geraniums, daisies, a buttercup in the water (but this I saw two or three

Daisies. 'There were flowers of various kinds . . .'

days before), small yellow flowers (I do not know their name) in the turf, a large bunch of strawberry blossoms. Wm. sate a while with me, then went to meet M. and S. Last Saturday I dined at Mr. Simpson's, also a beautiful mild day. Monday was a frosty day and it has been frost ever since. It is to-day Christmas Day, Saturday, 25th December 1802. I am thirty-one years of age. It is a dull, frosty day.

Again I have neglected to write my Journal — New Year's Day is passed, Old Christmas day and I have recorded nothing. It is today *Tuesday,* January 11th. On Christmas day I dressed myself ready to go [to] Keswick in a returned chaise, but did not go. On Thursday, 30th December, I went to K. William rode before me to the foot of the hill nearest K. There we parted close to a little watercourse, which was then noisy with water, but on my return a dry channel. We ate some potted beef on horseback and sweet cake. We stopped our horse close to the hedge, opposite a tuft of primroses, three flowers in full blossom and a bud. They reared themselves up among the green moss. We debated long whether we should pluck [them], and at last left them to live out their day, which I was right glad of at my return the Sunday following; for there they remained, uninjured either by cold or wet. I stayed at K. over New Year's Day, and returned on Sunday, the 2nd January. Wm. Mackareth fetched me — (M. and S. walked as far as John Stanley's) — Wm. was alarmed at my long delay, and came to within three miles of Keswick. He mounted before me. It had been a sweet mild day and was a pleasant evening. C. stayed with us till Tuesday, January 4th. Wm. and I walked up to George M.'s to endeavour to get the horse, then walked with him to Ambleside. We parted with him at the turning of the lane, he going on horseback

to the top of Kirkstone. On Thursday 6th, C. returned, and on Friday, the 7th, he and Sara went to Keswick. W. accompanied them to the foot of Wytheburn. I to Mrs. Simpson's, and dined, and called on Aggy Fleming sick in bed. It was a gentle day, and when Wm. and I returned home just before sunset, it was a heavenly evening. A soft sky was among the hills, and a summer sunshine above, blending with this sky, for it was more like sky than clouds. The turf looked warm and soft.

[*January*] *8th, Saturday*. Wm. and I walked to Rydale — no letters. Still as mild as spring — a beautiful moonlight evening and a quiet night, but before morning the wind rose, and it became dreadfully cold. We were not well, Mary and I.

[*January*] *9th, Sunday*. Mary lay long in bed and did not walk. Wm. and I walked in Brother's Wood. I was *astonished* with the beauty of the place for I had never been here since my return home — never since before I went away in June!! Wrote to Miss Lamb.

January 10th, 1803, Monday. I lay in bed to have a drench of sleep till one o'clock. Worked all day — petticoats — Mrs. C.'s wrists. Ran Wm.'s woollen stockings, for he put them on today for the first time. We walked to Rydale and brought letters from Sara, Annette and [?] — furiously cold.

January 11th, Tuesday. A very cold day. Wm. promised me he would rise as soon as I had carried him his breakfast, but he lay in bed till between 12 and 1. We talked of walking, but the blackness of the cold made us slow to put forward, and we did not walk at all. Mary read the Prologue to Chaucer's tales to me in the morning. William was working at his poem to C. Letter from Keswick and from Taylor on Wm.'s marriage. C. poorly, in bad spirits. Canaries. Before tea I sate 2 hours in the parlour. Read part of *The Knight's Tale* with exquisite delight. Since tea Mary has been down stairs copying out Italian poems for Stuart. William has been working beside me, and here ends this imperfect summary. I will take a nice Calais Book, and *will* for the future write regularly and, if I can, legibly; so much for this my resolution on *Tuesday* night, January 11th, 1803. Now I am going to take tapioca for my supper, and Mary an egg, William some cold mutton — his poor chest is tired.

[*January*] 12*th, Wednesday*. Very cold, and cold all the week.

[*January*] 16*th, Sunday*. Intensely cold. Wm. had a fancy for some ginger bread. I put on Molly's cloak and my Spenser, and we walked towards Matthew Newton's. I went into the house. The blind man and his wife and sister were sitting by the fire, all dressed very clean in their Sunday clothes, the sister reading. They took their little stock of gingerbread out of the cupboard, and I bought 6 pennyworth. They were so grateful when I paid them for it that I could not find it in my heart to tell them we were going to make gingerbread ourselves. I had asked them if they had no thick — "No," answered Matthew, "there was none on Friday, but we'll *endeavour* to get some." The next day the woman came just when we were baking and we bought 2 pennyworth.

THE ARTISTS

The Revd THOMAS AUSTIN was an amateur artist who made the sketches included here during visits to the Lake District in the 1830s and 1840s.

THOMAS BEWICK (1755–1828) was born at Newcastle-upon-Tyne, where he established a school of engraving. The bird engravings in this volume are taken from his illustrations for books of natural history.

THE BOTANICAL MAGAZINE or Flower Garden Displayed. The coloured flower illustrations in this book (apart from the dog rose) are taken from William Curtis's magazine, which began publication in 1787. The botanical engravings come from books of botany published in the early years of the nineteenth century by Longman, Hurst, Rees and Orme, Thomas Tegg, Baldwin and Cradock, and Nuttall, Fisher and Dixon.

WILLIAM COLLINS (1758–1847) was the son of an Irish art dealer and father of the novelist, Wilkie Collins. He knew Wordsworth through his friendship with Sir George Beaumont.

JOHN SELL COTMAN (1782–1842) was an important member of the Norwich School of painting. He founded a school for drawing in Norwich and later became Professor of Drawing at King's College, London.

JOHN GLOVER (1767–1849), born in Leicestershire, was a founder member of the Society of Painters in Watercolours. He was a frequent visitor to the Lakes and also very successful in selling his paintings of them. Later in life he emigrated to farm in Tasmania.

JOHN HARDEN (1772–1847) was born in County Tipperary. A man of independent means, he moved to Brathay Hall near Ambleside in 1804, a year after his marriage. He was a gifted amateur artist who gives us views of life in the Lake District not recorded by commercial artists. Most of his paintings in this book are reproduced here for the first time in colour.

WILLIAM HAVELL (1782–1857) was one of a family of painters. He painted subjects throughout Britain and in Italy, India and the Far East.

JULIUS CAESAR IBBETSON (1759–1817) was a Yorkshireman who established a reputation as a painter of country scenes. During the period of the *Journals* he lived firstly at Clappersgate, near Ambleside, and then at Troutbeck, between Ambleside and Windermere. Dorothy records drinking tea at this Clappersgate home on June 16th 1800 (page 36), and his painting of this home can be seen on pages 110–11.

PHILIPPE JACQUES DE LOUTHERBOURG (1740–1812) was born in Alsace and came to England in 1771, where he championed the idea of English landscape and scenery as subjects for painting.

WILLIAM HENRY PYNE (1769–1843) was a water-colour painter of landscape and figure subjects and published many works in conjunction with Ackermann. A selection of his innumerable studies of rustic figures and scenes is reproduced in this book.

PIERRE JOSEPH REDOUTÉ (1759–1840) was the most distinguished flower painter of the age. The dog-rose on page 35 is from his famous book, *Les Roses*.

RAMSEY RICHARD REINAGLE (1775–1862) was the son of Philip Reinagle and, like him, produced a prolific number of paintings in his career, mostly landscapes and scenes in England and Italy.

JAMES BURRELL SMITH was active in the middle of the nineteenth century. He was a native of Alnwick, Northumberland.

JOHN 'WARWICK' SMITH (1749–1831) was a landscape painter who benefited from the patronage of the Second Earl of Warwick.

JOSEPH MALLORD WILLIAM TURNER (1775–1851) was the great genius of English landscape painting in the nineteenth century. He worked at first exclusively in water-colour, but later in oil as well.

JOHN VARLEY (1778–1842) was a leading painter of landscapes in water-colours in the early nineteenth century.

WILLIAM WESTALL (1781–1850) was the brother of another painter, Richard. After disastrous journeys to the Far East and the West Indies, he returned to England to work mainly as a topographical water-colourist.

FRANCIS WHEATLEY (1747–1801) began his career as a portrait painter in London, but later specialized in rural and domestic scenes.

JOSEPH WRIGHT of Derby (1734–97) established himself as a portrait painter in Derby but travelled to Italy and also painted landscape studies in Dovedale and the Lake District.

ACKNOWLEDGEMENTS

The publishers and producers would like to thank the Trustees of the Estate of Ernest de Selincourt for permission to reproduce parts of the *Journals* first published by Mr. de Selincourt. Special thanks for their help are also due to Dr. Terry McCormack and Rosemary Hoggarth of the Dove Cottage Trust, Grasmere, Victoria Slowe and Cherrie Trelogan of Abbot Hall Art Gallery, Kendal, Paul Allonby, Don Brookes, Curator of Rydal Mount, Peter Jones of King's College, Cambridge, Peter Bicknell of Downing College, Cambridge and William Sandover. The museums, galleries, private collectors, artists, photographers, photographic agencies and institutions who kindly gave permission for their works to be reproduced in this book are:
Abbot Hall Art Gallery, Kendal: 13, 21, 26, 27, 31, 40, 45, 51, 52, 66, 79, 81, 89, 90, 91, 99, 101, 106, 113, 123, 125, 126–7, 133, 152, 155, 162, 182–3, 187, 211
Bodleian Library: (RRy 146(3)) 35, (2796 e 120) 78, (*Ibid.* 119) 97, (Per 19113 d 55. Vol. 21 Plate 2160) 59, (*Ibid.* Vol. 19 Plate 10) 119, (*Ibid.* Vol. 19 Plate 1221) 171, (*Ibid.* Vol. 18 Plate 63) 179, (*Ibid.* Vol. 27 Plate 2174) 215, (Gough 4° 295 Vol. 3) 197
British Museum: 17, 20, 25, 28, 29, 30, 32–3, 36, 37, 38–9, 42, 48–9, 56, 57, 60, 61, 64, 65, 68, 69, 76, 84–5, 86, 94, 104, 115, 117, 121, 128, 130–1, 144, 145, 148, 154, 158, 160, 161, 166, 169, 173, 176, 177, 184, 185, 189, 193, 201, 204, 207, 208–9, 213, 214, 216, 217
Carlisle Library: 73   Cornell University Library, William Wordsworth Collection: 11
Derby Art Gallery: 71, 143   Dover Museum: 200
The Trustees of the Faringdon Collection: 63
Ferens Art Gallery (Hull City Museums and Art Galleries): 74–5, 110–11
Fitzwilliam Museum, Cambridge: 147 (above)   The Fotomas Index: 67, 195
Government Art Collection: 54–5, 95, 190–1
King's College Library, Cambridge, Bicknell Collection: 43, 114, 138-9
The Laing Art Gallery, Newcastle-upon-Tyne, reproduction by permission of Tyne and Wear Museums Service: 87
Leeds City Art Galleries: 22–3   David Mckeown: 18
National Portrait Gallery, London: 14   Andy Newton: 202
Private Collections. Photographs by courtesy of Christie's: 102–3, 150–1
Royal Holloway College. Photograph by courtesy of The Bridgeman Art Library: 47
The Tate Gallery, London: 159, 205
Victoria and Albert Museum: 2–3, 109, 137, 156   Richard Wordsworth: 6
Yale Center for British Art, Paul Mellon Collection: 167, 175, 198–9

INDEX